# LIGHTING
# THEIR FIRES

# LIGHTING THEIR FIRES

Raising Extraordinary Kids in
a Mixed-up, Muddled-up,
Shook-up World

## RAFE ESQUITH

VIKING

VIKING
Published by the Penguin Group
Penguin Group (USA) Inc., 375 Hudson Street, New York, New York 10014, U.S.A.
Penguin Group (Canada), 90 Eglinton Avenue East, Suite 700, Toronto, Ontario,
Canada M4P 2Y3 (a division of Pearson Penguin Canada Inc.)
Penguin Books Ltd, 80 Strand, London WC2R 0RL, England
Penguin Ireland, 25 St. Stephen's Green, Dublin 2, Ireland (a division of Penguin Books Ltd)
Penguin Books Australia Ltd, 250 Camberwell Road, Camberwell, Victoria 3124, Australia
(a division of Pearson Australia Group Pty Ltd)
Penguin Books India Pvt Ltd, 11 Community Centre, Panchsheel Park,
New Delhi—110 017, India
Penguin Group (NZ), 67 Apollo Drive, Rosedale, North Shore 0632, New Zealand
(a division of Pearson New Zealand Ltd)
Penguin Books (South Africa) (Pty) Ltd, 24 Sturdee Avenue, Rosebank,
Johannesburg 2196, South Africa

Penguin Books Ltd, Registered Offices: 80 Strand, London WC2R 0RL, England

First published in 2009 by Viking Penguin, a member of Penguin Group (USA) Inc.

1  3  5  7  9  10  8  6  4  2

Grateful acknowledgment is made for permission to reprint an excerpt from *Oh, The Places
You'll Go!* by Dr. Seuss. TM & copyright © by Dr. Seuss Enterprises L.P., 1990. Used by
permission of Random House Children's Books, a division of Random House, Inc.

LIBRARY OF CONGRESS CATALOGING-IN-PUBLICATION DATA
Esquith, Rafe.
Lighting their fires : raising extraordinary kids in a mixed-up, muddled-up,
shook-up world / Rafe Esquith.
p. cm.
ISBN 978-0-670-02108-6
1. Child rearing—United States.  2. Education—United States—Philosophy.  3. Motivation
in education—United States.  4. Values—Study and teaching—United States.  I. Title.
HQ778.63.E87 2009
649'.1—dc22          2009008327

Printed in the United States of America

for all who work to make a difference
and for Barbara

# Contents

# LIGHTING
# THEIR FIRES

# Out of the Ordinary

It was five P.M. on a Friday afternoon in May at Hobart Elementary School in Los Angeles, and most of the dedicated teachers and administrators had long since left the campus. I wished I could have escaped with them. I was exceedingly tired. It had been a particularly long week. In fact, it had been a long year.

Yet, this Friday I was able to push myself even though a long night lay ahead of me. A few months before, I had spoken to some outstanding teachers at a school in Los Angeles. One of them was friends with the general manager of the Los Angeles Dodgers baseball team. When she learned of my love of baseball, she called him to arrange tickets. He graciously offered my class six tickets for several games during the year. I would be able to take five kids per game, and after picking names out of a hat, a schedule was made to ensure that eventually all the kids in the class would get to attend a contest. So on this Friday night, five students were coming with me to attend their first baseball game. It would be a fun night, but also a late one.

On Saturday mornings I normally work with my former students, a group of enthusiastic teenagers who return to prepare for college admissions tests and read the plays of William Shakespeare. Probably more tired than I, these hard-working scholars sacrifice most of their Saturday mornings to come back to Room 56 once more. Many of them yearn for a more relevant education than they are receiving at the schools they currently attend. But this was the Friday before Memorial Day weekend, so I had given them (and myself) a Saturday off. I was truly exhausted, but I consoled myself knowing that after the ball game ended I could go home and get a good night's sleep.

Outside my classroom, I could see the crooked parking lot gates struggling to remain open. This sixteen-foot-high fence has two pieces that swing shut and can be bolted with a large padlock and chain. It's unfortunate that we even need this contraption, but the school is in a rough neighborhood, and keeping the kids and their resources safe is a big priority. Unfortunately, it is plain to see that the barricade is in real need of repair. Over the years it has been damaged by cars, climbers, and rain, so that the two swinging sections do not remain apart when they are supposed to and are difficult to close when it's time to lock up the school. Like the facilities they guard, the gates do the best they can under difficult circumstances.

Inside, though, the environment can seem like a different world. On this Friday, as on all Friday afternoons, a group of amazing fourth and fifth graders had stayed late with me in Room 56. They were part of the Hobart Shakespeareans group, and had been working on an unabridged production of William

Shakespeare's *As You Like It*. The previous summer, these kids had volunteered to come to school through July and August to dissect the play's intricate language, learn accompanying parts on musical instruments, and unite for a cause that would bring hope to themselves and those around them. After eleven months of rehearsals, the kids were ready to perform the production for the public. They knew their show was brilliant. Just a few months earlier the Royal Shakespeare Company had spent the day with them and wept and cheered through an unforgettable performance.

School officially ended that Friday at 2:19 P.M., but these children had volunteered to stay daily until 5:00. As they said their good-byes, threw on their backpacks, and headed out the door, six of them stayed behind. Five were going with me to the Dodgers game, and they were understandably excited. But the sixth, Sammy, was not, and I quickly grew concerned.

When I first met Sammy, he was not popular with his teachers or classmates, and it was easy to see why. He couldn't sit still in class. He often spoke out of turn and rarely interrupted with a point that was even remotely relevant to the topic of conversation.

In addition, he was filthy. He was unwashed and his clothes were even worse. It wasn't that his personal habits were bad; he simply didn't have any. On the playground, he would take off his shirt, throw it on the dirty blacktop, and work up a terrific sweat running. At Hobart, kids know never to leave anything on the ground, because any unattended backpack or article of clothing disappears within seconds of being left alone. But no one ever touched Sam's clothes. No one even wanted to go near them. After his activities were finished, Sam would pick up his shirt, use it to wipe the sweat off his face, and then put it back on. It wasn't a pretty sight.

Sam didn't have friends among his peers or even supporters on the staff, and yet he and I slowly developed a friendship. Always on the outside looking in, Sam had spent his first nine years following the path of least resistance. Never a joiner of anything, he had eventually signed on to many of the extra activities I offered. He was the final kid in the class to begin staying late for Shakespeare. Over early-morning math lessons, lunchtime music sessions, and playing lots of catch, Sam had made tremendous progress. He discovered that he loved United States history, and once he found his great interest, a scholar was born. He devoured every book he could find on the subject, with a particular focus on the politics of war. His patriotic passion overflowed into his life. Sammy became more organized in his thinking. He started keeping himself clean. Now, after eleven months in the class, Sam was one of the gang. He had a lot of genuine friends, and he never felt better.

But on this Friday night, he was depressed. He loved baseball, and I had to leave him behind from the game he desperately wanted to attend. He knew he would go to a game later that summer, but he was sad that he couldn't go that night. Spending an evening at Dodger Stadium obviously appealed to him more than being at home.

Sam told me his mother would be coming to get him around five-thirty and asked if he could remain in the room after I left. I wanted to say yes but I had been reprimanded several times by my bosses for allowing kids to stay late and study in Room 56 after I had gone home. I understood their concerns. Although the administrators trusted my students to do the right thing, they were worried about liability problems, and told me to discontinue the practice. As a classroom teacher with enough battles on my hands, I was more than happy to relent on this point and save my strength for more important issues. Sam promised me his mom was coming on the bus, and he sat on a playground bench near our classroom while he waited. The sun was shining, and although the ubiquitous gangsters had already taken over the basketball courts, there would be daylight for at least another two hours. I was confident that Sammy, the budding historian, would be okay.

Even on Friday at five P.M., challenges like this face teachers who put in the extra mile. With Sam squared away, I could turn my attention back to the ball game in our future.

A few minutes later, a quintet of fifth graders piled into my van, dubbed the Oprahmobile by my former students. Oprah was incredibly kind to help out my class several years ago and we will be forever grateful for her generosity. The children were simply giddy. They were going to their first game and were well prepared. They had played baseball daily on the school playground, and I taught them to score games in October when we watched the World Series on television. The Ken Burns baseball documentary was required viewing during their spring vacation evenings. Now, after a year's preparation, they were going to watch professionals play the sport they had grown to love. In addition, the Dodgers had kindly invited the children to visit their offices before the game to learn about the business of baseball. As an added treat, they were to be taken onto the field to watch batting practice before taking their seats for the game.

We arrived at the Dodgers' headquarters and were told by a friendly but firm security officer to wait until an official had cleared our admittance. Soon, we were met by our tour guide. She was courteous, but it was plain to see she was tired. She had probably led children on tours for many years, and I could tell by her eyes that this was about the last thing she wanted to do on a Friday evening. Don't get me wrong—the guide was perfectly nice when she introduced herself, but one sensed she had met enough disinterested and hyperactive children to douse any enthusiasm she might have had about leading yet another group of kids through Dodgers history.

And then something wonderful happened. It's the kind of moment I live for. It's why I love being both a parent and a teacher.

Our guide said, "Let's get started," and we entered the Dodgers' command center. She proceeded to march us down a long corridor past several offices, but the kids stopped short when they noticed something in the passageway. Hanging on the wall was a picture of a famous movie star from Hollywood's Golden Age who happened to be an ardent Dodgers fan. It was a wonderful photograph, taken at least forty years ago, showing him sitting in the stands at Dodger Stadium, rooting for his team.

"Hey, look!" exclaimed Cesar. "It's Henry Fonda." All of the kids had recognized him, but Cesar, the leader of this particular group, gave voice to the thought they were sharing.

"You know Henry Fonda?" asked the guide, stunned that a fifth grader knew of an actor who had died a quarter of a century ago. Suddenly, her eyes were no longer tired. She was truly surprised and curious.

"Sure," said Cesar. "Henry Fonda . . . star of *12 Angry Men,* a great 1957 film by Sidney Lumet. But I liked him even better in *The Grapes of Wrath.* I think John Ford did a fantastic job putting Steinbeck on film. Did you like *The Grapes of Wrath?* We saw an incredible production at Ford's Theatre last year."

At this, a couple of heads poked out of the various rooms. Nothing was said, but from that moment on we had a transformed tour guide. She asked challenging questions, and the tour that we were told would last about ten minutes took almost an hour. After the kids expressed their appreciation and left to buy hot dogs before the game began, our happy but mystified guide pulled me aside.

"I don't really know what to say to you," she said haltingly, "but your kids are unlike any other group I have ever taken around. They're so confident but so sweet. They're so beautiful and they glow." She paused, searching for the right adjective.

"They're extraordinary," she said in almost whispered respect.

I'm fortunate to hear this a lot, and that's what this book is about. From airport terminals to Shakespeare festivals to hotel lobbies, people stop, stare, and speak up. And the praise goes beyond "What a wonderfully behaved group of children you have." These kids are distinctive, a quality all the more remarkable given that our society often seems bent on preventing anyone from walking to the beat of a different drummer.

But here's the secret. These students weren't born extraordinary— they *became* that way. This is the central theme of this book. These wonderful children didn't always glow or know about Henry Fonda. There was a time when fractions were a mystery and Shakespeare a boring dead white man. But they had been exposed to these concepts and ideals by a series of fine teachers, and had them reinforced by parents who understood how important they were to their kids' development.

Children are born with varying levels of talent and intelligence, but possessing natural smarts and skills is no guarantee of success. It takes more than that: it takes work on the part of parents and teachers to cultivate these qualities, to instill in children the drive and character necessary to translate their natural gifts into extraordinary results. There was a time when these children at Dodger Stadium had been only diamonds in the rough, and not the shimmering gems that delighted their guide. Over the years they had been polished by caring and wise adults. And here's the great news: with patient guidance your child can glow as well. It takes great sacrifice, effort, and preparation to make this journey with your kid. It's a hard road, one that many parents and children ultimately find too demanding to pursue. But as Robert Frost taught us, the road less traveled can make all the difference.

In Rome, kind Italians warn visitors that traffic lights are just suggestions. That's what you are about to read: suggestions. I've been teaching for almost thirty years and have watched my own children grow up. And I've come to one realization: there isn't one right way to raise children. There are countless points of view and many of them are valid and interesting. Yet, I have also come to understand why I take children out on a Friday night when I am too tired to do so. I want to help children become special. I know that every day matters. I have come to realize that even one night at a baseball game might be the moment a child decides to be unique. Children are capable of learning astonishing things in the most unexpected places. With our help and patience, the cure for cancer or the next great novel might be sitting next to us at a ball game. And there are steps we can actively take to help children reach the kind of excellence that we dream about for them.

I fear something for all the children I have been blessed to know, and it's not drugs or gangs. I fear that my children will be *mediocre,* that they won't live up to the tremendous promise that each of them possesses. I don't want my children to be mediocre, because I know they are capable of more. So let the polishing begin.

Play ball.

# The Readiness Is All

The first pitch was a called strike and the game was under way. The children were especially amazed by the sound of the ball hitting the catcher's mitt. They also couldn't help but appreciate their view of the field. At public events, children are often seated behind taller adults, and have to contort their bodies at various angles to find a good line of sight. But tonight there was no such problem. The three rows immediately in front of us were completely empty, even though it was a beautiful Friday evening at a stadium that normally draws some of the largest crowds in baseball.

"Where is everyone?" Austin asked me.

Having attended games at Dodger Stadium since 1962, I knew that the empty seats would fill up eventually. The ticket holders were simply late. But this magnified an important concept that is too often overlooked in the raising of children. Our kids must understand the concept of time, and this begins with the importance of being *on* time.

On most report cards, teachers give some sort of grade based on a student's ability to "make good use of time." But what does that really mean? In most cases, it is merely an evaluation of whether a child has stayed on task and finished an assignment.

The grade has nothing to say about whether children learn the *relevance* of time. Some might wonder why a little kid would need to have the faintest idea about time and its importance, but this attitude can be fatal to a child's development of good life habits. Children must understand that a person who appreciates time will be able to do exceptional things with his life.

The Cardinals went out quickly in the top of the first, and the middle of the inning provided an opportunity to address Austin's question.

RAFE:      People will be coming, Austin. They're late for the game. It happens a lot. Dodger fans are infamous for being late for games.

AUSTIN:  Then they miss some of the game!

RAFE:      Yes, they do.

CESAR:   But they won't know what happened.

RAFE:      Well, they check the score.

CESAR:   But they won't really understand what's going on. When the Cardinals who came up in the first come up again, they won't have seen how the Dodgers pitched to them the first time around. A score doesn't tell you everything.

RAFE:      I agree with you, Cesar. That's why we come on time.

JESSICA: It's not nice to the players, either.

Children need to learn that it is essential to be on time. It's a way of life. During their lives, they will be faced with all sorts of deadlines. Whether writing a report for a school assignment or filling out an application for a scholarship, being on time matters. Being punctual requires planning. Before we went to the Dodger game, the kids and I discussed what time we should leave our school. We had to take into account that traffic in Los Angeles is terrible, especially on a Friday evening. When we were in the van the kids and I laughed at the GPS, which told us that with three miles to go to the stadium, we should be there in about six minutes. Even ten-year-olds who have lived in the City of Angels know better than that.

We had talked about the kindness of the Dodger officials who had given us tickets and were preparing to give us a tour of the offices at 5:45 P.M. If we were late, it would be disrespectful to all the people who had worked hard to give us this opportunity. It would also be rude to the kind woman who contacted the Dodgers in the first place to set up our evening at the stadium. Being on time reflects an appreciation of others, something many people overlook.

Not everyone appreciates this, of course. When my class performs a Shakespeare play every year in Room 56, we run the show as a professional theater. Latecomers have to wait for a break in the action before they are seated. The children are taught that when people come late to a play, they disturb the people who came on time. It's not pleasant to be interrupted by someone crawling over you to get to his seat. Some tardy guests become very upset with our policy. Some have yelled at or written nasty letters to the class. It's good for the kids to experience this; they learn from observing the behavior of others. There is no need to pull them aside and tell them, "You've just witnessed something that you might consider when establishing your own system of values."

The students have noticed a direct correlation between being late to an event and the propensity to engage in generally thoughtless behavior. They have pointed out in class discussions that a cell phone that went off during a performance usually belonged to a person who arrived late. The children learn firsthand that a lack of respect for being on time is a good indicator of more pervasive insensitivity.

The same lesson can be learned at an airport if you travel with your children. Surely no one is happy with air travel these days, what with security lines and delayed flights. Still, it's amazing that every time my students and I are waiting to go through a metal detector, we see TSA workers being screamed at by passengers in line whose flights are leaving in fifteen minutes. As children who have been taught the importance of being on time, the kids realize that the furious passengers could have avoided the situation by being at the airport earlier. This is a consistent lesson young people can learn: those who are late often take out their frustrations on people who have nothing to do with their misfortune. Being on time reflects a belief that we can control our own destiny, and that we are responsible for our actions.

Point out to children that adults expect others to be on time. People get upset if someone is late for an appointment. Everyone would be furious if a doctor were late for surgery. Being responsible means holding oneself to the same standard of punctuality, and this process should be learned in childhood.

## Using Weekends to Teach Time Management

The late, great George Carlin often ridiculed soccer moms for overprogramming their kids, and many people completely agree with him. As someone who does not believe in lots of homework, I too think children need some time to do nothing. They need time to play in the mud, look at the clouds, and process all the information they are receiving, especially now, when that information is coming at a faster pace than ever before.

But there is a problem. Many kids, when left to their own devices, with limited experiences and abilities, will make poor choices. If we leave children alone for hours at a time, a television or computer screen can become a frighteningly dangerous enemy, sapping away valuable time with frivolous and numbing distractions. The key is to find a happy medium in which our children are not overprogrammed by us or by what they're watching if we're not around.

Here is a little exercise I do on Friday afternoons with my students. The children and I sit down and take a look at the hours in a weekend, and we discuss how they will spend their time. My students are devotees of J.R.R. Tolkien's *The Lord of the Rings*,  and before the weekend begins, we remember the wizard Gandalf's sage advice: "All you have to do is to decide what to do with the time given to you."

Parents can do this on a sheet of paper, but I do it up on a board that the entire class can see:

5:00 P.M.: We leave school on Friday.

6:30 A.M.: We will be back in school for Math Team the following Monday.

Hours:     61.5 hours of time to spend

Sleep:     9 hours per night for 3 nights=27 hours

At this point the children subtract to find that they have 34.5 hours of time on the weekend to use or waste. They estimate that they will spend approximately 6 hours eating meals and doing chores such as cleaning the house. They now have 28.5 hours left.

I then ask them to estimate the amount of time they will spend doing a family activity such as seeing relatives or going to church. Even the most programmed children will come up with, at most, ten hours on an average weekend. This means they still have more than eighteen hours left.

I ask the kids to consider the following information. Even if they want to spend thirteen hours just fooling around—be it playing tag, watching movies, riding a bike, talking about who likes whom, or napping in the park and listening to the hum of insects—they still have five hours remaining to read or study.

That's five hours to think about the coming week and get a head start on a particular project; five hours to read _The Chronicles of Narnia,_ not because it has been assigned but because they love it; or five hours to help a neighbor in need. Regardless of a child's personal choices, with direction a young person can be shown the importance of time. Not every second has to be programmed, but with guidance a young person can envision a weekend more clearly and use the days effectively instead of sitting on a couch for twelve hours watching television and waking up Monday morning regretting the lost time.

## For Classroom Teachers

Teachers can model effective time management. At the elementary level, where classrooms are often self-contained, instructors have an opportunity to be either wasteful or efficient with their day. If, for example, a morning consists of a reading and a math session, it's fun to practice with your students how long it takes them to put away their reading materials and get ready for numbers. This is not to suggest a whirlwind of one set of books being thrown into desks while another is ripped out. But many classrooms take too much time between lessons. Here is a shocking fact: students can waste hundreds of hours a year merely changing subjects. These valuable hours, if recovered, could be spent reading great literature or solving math questions. At many urban elementary schools, where more than half the children cannot pass basic reading and math tests, there is clearly no time to waste.

For high school teachers, the situation is even more difficult. With students entering and leaving the class hourly, a fifty-two-minute class may in fact be only forty-nine minutes long. It's essential for students to understand that three wasted minutes translate to an hour of missed learning opportunities per month. The best high school teachers value every second they can spend with their students, and burn from the word go.

## Middle of the First

The Cardinals did not score in the top of the first. While the huge stadium screen blasted music and force-fed its captive audience commercials from the latest Hollywood drivel, the kids summarized the inning. On their score sheets, they tabulated runs, hits, errors, and men left on base.

A latecomer walked down our aisle. He was actually sitting several rows in front of us, but because there were still many empty seats, he stopped by our group on his way down and poked Jin Uk.

LATECOMER: Did I miss anything?
JIN UK: A lot. [The little professor is always honest.]
LATECOMER: What's the score?
JIN UK: Zero-zero. Dodgers are coming up.
LATECOMER: So I didn't miss anything

The man was relieved and went happily to his seat.

It often seems that we live in a "bottom line" society, where the final score or final grade is all that matters. Exceptional children grow to understand that the journey is everything. It's wonderful to get an A on an exam, but even better to reflect on the studying and learning that led up to the grade. It's exciting to perform a play or concert and hear the cheers from a live audience, but extraordinary children know that the thousands of hours spent rehearsing are actually more meaningful and joyous than the performance itself.

Simply by being on time, these children gave themselves a chance to understand more of the action on the field. Those arriving late hadn't missed any scoring, but the score alone did not reflect the depth of what had occurred. In one-half of an inning, the Dodger pitcher had established his game plan for the night, and the Cardinals had as well. The kids saw whether the Cardinals were swinging at first pitches or working their way deep into the count. Both managers had selected certain players from a larger pool of talent, trying to gain an advantage for their team and giving them the best chance of winning the game. Outstanding players may have been passed over because the manager wanted to create a certain matchup. Being on time increased the children's understanding of the event, and that's a good thing.

## Lost in Translation

In John Sturges's *The Magnificent Seven,* the great remake of  Akira Kurosawa's film *Seven Samurai,* there is a marvelous moment when a gunfighter named Harry Luck believes he will receive huge amounts of gold for helping desperate Mexican farmers fight off a group of murderous bandits. It's not the case at all. Harry, played by Brad Dexter, will not listen even when Yul Brynner's character, Chris, warns him there is absolutely no pot of gold at the end of this rainbow.

There will always be people who hear what they want to hear, even if what they believe they have heard does not remotely resemble the original message. This is the *lost-in-translation syndrome.* Many schools have read or heard that the students in

Room 56 work hard, and in trying to replicate this success have turned their classrooms into Dickensian workhouses. Room 56 is also filled with laughter and joy, which is just as important. Still, some teachers with the best of intentions wind up playing Mr. Bumble to their students' Oliver Twist.

## Bottom of the First

The Dodgers were coming to bat, and Cesar, who believes that heaven must consist of a twenty-four-hour-a-day baseball game, was frustrated. He saw people at the game not enjoying or appreciating the opportunity to watch amazing athletes. As a young man who frequently invokes "carpe diem" (seize the day) as his personal motto, it is puzzling for this marvelous but still ten-year-old mind to fathom that people might be unaware of the names of the teams they are watching, let alone untutored on the finer points of baseball.

Let's be clear about something. There is *nothing wrong* with going to a ball game to have a beer and relax after a hard day's work. No one should be required to watch the action or care about anyone's batting average. It's an individual choice.

But my job is to help little ones see beyond the surface, and to use their time in such a way as to gain a deeper understanding of the world around them. It is one way, but not the only way, to raise a child. And it is far from joyless. Children are capable of having fantastic fun while spending their time wisely. The two concepts do not have to be mutually exclusive. There are many people in our society, possibly the majority, who might describe *fun* as screaming and/or throwing food while mugging for a camera. If that's their definition of *fun,* so be it. But as long as parents want something more for a child, they need to use a different dictionary.

## The Bigger Picture

Children need to be taught to be on time, but this message is just the beginning. Once a fundamental idea is introduced, its message is forever expanding. The first lesson is to always be on time. While many people may not agree with the importance of this statement, and may even laugh at themselves or their families for being chronically late, punctuality should be a starting point when working with kids. However, as children learn to be on time, they also have the opportunity to see how the concept of time, whether considered in a geographical or a historical context, plays a major part in their lives.

It was the bottom of the first with one out. The lights came on in the stadium because the sky had turned a shade of gray. Ye Rim looked back and forth from the action at the plate to the various scoreboards of the stadium that flashed the score, count, and pitch speed. On the outfield wall she noticed all sorts of cities and numbers. She was confused. There were dozens of numbers and, to make matters more puzzling, they changed constantly.

YE RIM: What are those numbers on the outfield wall?

RAFE:  Oh, those are the scores from all the games being played around the country tonight.

YE RIM: Why are the numbers different in left field than right field?

RAFE:     The scores over there are the National League teams
          and the other ones are the American League teams.
          Remember how we studied the different divisions?
          They divide up the scores by divisions and change
          the numbers as the scores change throughout the
          evening. Understand?

YE RIM: No.

RAFE:     Sure, you do. It's easy, Yo Yo [my pet name for the
          diminutive singer]. You can see the Red Sox are
          winning, four-to-two, while the Diamondbacks
          and Giants are tied, zero-zero. What don't you
          understand about that?

YE RIM: I see the scores. But why do the Red Sox have
          more numbers than the Giants?

RAFE:     Because the Red Sox are in the eighth inning and
          the Giants' game has barely begun.

*Flash.* In learning about time, the door had just been opened
to teach a child a very important point. Time is relative. Ye Rim
had traveled to other time zones and understood that, for example, Washington, D.C. , is three hours ahead of Los Angeles. But
the little girl, as bright as she is, had not yet owned this concept.
She still thought that everything in the world happened at the
same time, and she didn't realize that games on the East Coast
had begun hours before the Giants' game being played in San
Francisco. Once she grasped this, Ye Rim had fun watching the
scoreboard all night long. She became fascinated with the fact
that Kansas City was playing the same game at a different time
than the Yankees, and that the players from those teams would
probably be in bed as the Dodgers and Cardinals continued to

battle at Dodger Stadium. Because of the focus on time, Ye Rim began to take an interest in geography, and time zones, and the relativity of it all. And all this while the Dodgers batted in the bottom of the first.

In the months to come, this little girl would travel often to perform around the nation. She always reset her watch when boarding a plane. She wanted to plan out her day as she passed through the time zones, and had learned how to do so while watching baseball scores flash on the Dodger Stadium wall.

## The Biggest Picture

Eventually an understanding of the relativity of time leads to the most important development of all—an interest in history, and in what it has to tell us about the present. Children today often have no understanding of history's importance. In fact, it's not uncommon for teachers to proudly proclaim that they do not teach about "dead white men" in their history classes. This is a mistake. History matters, even the dead white men.

When it comes to studying history, there is something that makes extraordinary students different from many of their peers, and it is not intelligence or talent. Because they have developed a time-centered mentality, these young people grow to understand and *respect* other times. I am often asked, "How do you get your kids to like Shakespeare or Twain?" "Why do your kids enthusiastically play Vivaldi when mine want to hear only hip-hop or rock?" "Why do your children love *Casablanca*?" The answer is simple. It's because the Hobart Shakespeareans have learned to respect time and those who came before them. They have too much perspective on the past to believe that we live in the "now" and that nothing else matters. Children with a respect for time realize that the measure of anything great is that it has passed the *test* of time. They know that the latest pop star might sell millions of CDs, but the important question is whether people will be listening to this music in ten, fifty, or one hundred years. The odds say likely not. There is a reason the opening notes of Beethoven's Fifth Symphony are so familiar. The piece is universal and brilliant, as time has proven—the music has continued to move and influence people for hundreds of years. Children can think deeply enough to understand that all time is connected. A child who learns that the past has created the present and that the present will shape the future will be willing to explore other times beyond his own limited existence.

Extraordinary children embrace arts and people and ideas from across the ages, and they do so because of their love and respect for time. They don't see the events of the past as static or held at arm's length by the distance of years. And they don't think of the 1800s as strange or alien as they laugh hysterically when Tom Sawyer plans the slaughter of more innocents while the kids of St. Petersburg whitewash the fence for him. They see the merits of Twain's writing, translated through time, and they find *The Adventures of Tom Sawyer* incredibly funny. When we begin our study of Shakespeare, we remember praise from the poet Ben Jonson, who described the Bard as a man "not of an age, but for all time."

Another way to help kids engage with ideas from the past is to show them the geologic clock. A Google search of this term will lead you to many Web sites that show the ages of Earth's existence superimposed over a twenty-four-hour time period. Young people are shocked to see that if Earth time is measured over the period of one day, human existence does not begin until just a few seconds before midnight. In that context, Chaucer and Bach don't seem old anymore—they are just a millisecond away from us in time! The geologic clock helps children open their minds to those that came before, and in doing so take advantage of all the past has to offer.

## The Backpack

Most parents help their young children get ready for school. They buy school supplies and, particularly in a child's early years, help them organize their backpacks. Pencils, notebooks, and a cornucopia of other educational goodies are purchased in the often desperate effort of caring parents to prepare their child for learning. Our little soldiers need to be ready for battle, so to speak.

Parents can help their kids fill an extraordinary backpack with tools that will help them reach greater heights. Pencils and erasers are important, of course, but the truly essential tools are the products of knowledge they carry in their intellectual backpack. These are the tools that they use to navigate through life, and the lessons these tools impart are crystallized in films, books, games, hobbies, the wisdom of parents and teachers, and the children's own experiences. These tools are much more important than simply having the right calculator or laptop. During each inning of this book, a few simple suggestions will be made about what our children should carry around as they set out on what can often be the confusing and dangerous paths in front of them.

It is important to note that some of these tools are not easily acquired or grasped. In this respect, the elements of real success have little to do with the things children are currently being taught in class. Schools often make the false assumption that skills can be taught quickly and efficiently. Let's take a little glimpse behind the scenes.

These days, many well-meaning school districts bring together teachers, coaches, curriculum supervisors, and a cast of thousands to determine what skills your child needs to be successful. Once these "standards" have been established, pacing plans are then drawn up to make sure that each particular skill is taught at the same rate and in the same way to all children. This is, of course, absurd. It gets even worse when one considers the very real fact that nothing of value is learned permanently by a child in a day or two.

For example, in the Los Angeles Unified School District, fifth graders are supposed to learn the concept of nouns when studying grammar. It is safe to say that most people would agree that this is a good thing. By understanding nouns, a child will be a better writer and communicator of ideas. The sad fact, however, is that the district uses a workbook in which the children spend only about two days covering nouns. Supervisors walk around classrooms to make sure the teachers are doing their jobs. Weekly meetings are then held, and the supervisors, with a cleverly planned presentation and checklist, document that nouns have been taught and that the kids now know all about them.

Ridiculous.

As all parents know, children do not learn this way. Most kids, even very bright ones, need constant review and practice to truly own a concept in grammar, math, or science. In schools today, on paper it may appear that kids are learning skills, but in reality they are only renting them, soon to forget what they've learned over the weekend or summer vacation.

What this means for parents is that reinforcing the lessons taught in school (and adding a few of your own) is crucial in bolstering your child's understanding of essential concepts. This will take steady repetition and plenty of patience. In teaching your child the importance of time, please note that there will never be a moment when your child exclaims, "Aha! I have it! I never before considered the importance of time, but thanks to your outstanding example, I get it! Thank you, oh wise parent, for making my life better." If raising children were only that simple. Unfortunately, it's not. But if you are willing to hammer home this concept through frequently pointing out examples and having casual conversations on the subject (well timed, of course) your child will start to gain some knowledge that might not be covered in the classroom. Pointing out that baseball scores coming in from across the nation are from games being played in different time zones is just one easy example. Here are a few more specific lessons on time that should be a part of any child's education.

## Timely Readings

When it comes to literature, every child should read Thornton
Wilder's classic play *Our Town*, winner of the Pulitzer Prize. It is a magnificent work, good enough to be read several times over the course of childhood. Even young children are ready to read this with their families. The middle school years are a great time

to read it again, and high school study of it should be essential. Better still, have your children read the play before they attend a good production of it. There are several outstanding film versions available on DVD. Many people love the original 1940 film adaptation with William Holden and Martha Scott, but others prefer the excellent 1977 Hallmark Hall of Fame production with Hal Holbrook as the Stage Manager, supported by an all-star cast including Ned Beatty, Ronny Cox, Sada Thompson, Barbara Bel Geddes, and Robbie Benson.

Wilder's play is filled with brilliant speeches about time, discussing the families who once lived in Babylon and the Civil War boys who died for their country, "though they had never seen more than twenty miles of it themselves." Most important of all, make sure your kids understand the significance of Emily's journey back in time after her death. She realizes too late how little we appreciate the time we are given in this life, and this leads to her tearful question to the Stage Manager:

EMILY:                    Do any human beings realize life, while
                         they live it? Every, every minute?
STAGE MANAGER: No, the saints and poets—maybe they
                         do some.

Would it be such a terrible world if we raised saints and poets? It's an admirable goal to challenge students to live life, every, every minute. *Our Town* can be at the center of a young mind's appreciation of time.

For students who are ready for some real fire in their reading,  Alex Haley's brilliant book *The Autobiography of Malcolm X* can be read and supplemented with Spike Lee's sensational film

<u>Malcolm X</u>. Malcolm, knowing his days were numbered, always  wore a watch. He wrote that he never measured anything in distance but in time. He was always ten minutes from a place and never two miles. He lived by his watch, and indeed, you can see his ever-present timepiece in almost every photograph taken of him. Whether you agree with his politics or not, the book is brilliant, and Malcolm's musings on time are a good thing for a child to keep in mind when considering time in his own life.

## Hooray for Hollywood

*Before You Hit Play*

Watching films with young children and even older ones can be a fantastic learning experience for them. However, the key is to watch *with* your kids. Many of the films I watch with young people have some serious adult themes, and are often avoided by concerned parents who take a different view as to whether kids should be exposed to war, sex, and other mature matters of consequence. Most of the films I discuss here I have watched with my own children and continue to watch with students in my class. They are thought-provoking, and that's the point. But it's necessary for us to be there to guide our kids when their thinking is provoked.

*Spending Time at the Movies*

For fun, the family can make an entertaining ritual of spending each February 2 watching the uproarious movie *Groundhog Day*,  starring Bill Murray. Like all truly great comedies, the film uses humor to explore serious themes, in this case imagining the opportunity to have endless chances to learn from our mistakes and correct them. After the film, take a moment to remind your children that life is not like this—we often have only one chance to do the right thing and need to take advantage of every opportunity.

 For a bolder attempt to drive home the message, try screening George Pal's earnest 1960s version of H. G. Wells's novel *The Time Machine.* This film, starring Rod Taylor, Alan Young, and Yvette Mimieux, re-creates a past/future time relationship and has much to say about how all times are interrelated. As with most films, it is not as good as its source material, but the book can be part of a family reading project undertaken before watching the movie. In the film, the character H. G. Wells travels to the future to begin a new world, taking three books with him. His best friend is left behind and finds three empty spaces in the bookcase. It is never revealed which books Wells took on his journey to start the society. The viewer is asked to consider what three books he would choose to start a new civilization. Not only is the story exciting and entertaining, but it also challenges a child to consider how our present knowledge might shape our future. Parents are often frustrated with their children because they reject the past and refuse to think about the future. *The Time Machine* is one addition to the backpack that can motivate a child to begin looking in both directions.

 Finally, make sure your child watches *Amadeus*, Milos Forman's 1984 film that took home best picture honors at the Academy Awards. Early in the film, there is a wonderful moment when a priest tries to console the composer Salieri, who has recently attempted suicide. Salieri plays several musical pieces he had long ago composed and becomes increasingly depressed as the priest recognizes none of them, despite the fact that they were all once "hit" tunes. Finally, Salieri plays a piece that the priest immediately recognizes (as will your child). The priest tries to compliment the depressed composer by saying he had no idea that his patient had written this famous piece of music.

"I didn't," moans the frustrated Salieri, and it's true—the piece was written by his contemporary and competitor, Mozart. It's a great scene from a wonderful production, and good for a child to consider. We recognize Mozart's music hundreds of years after his death because it has passed the test of time, and this scene serves as a funny and important reminder of that concept.

## If Music Be the Food of Love, Play On

The world would be a better place if playing music was a requirement for every child on the planet. Music is crucial for a child's complete development no matter his aptitude. For many reasons, kids who play music have a better understanding of time than those who do not.

Einstein wrote about the connection between music and math, and students who perform brilliantly in music often develop a love of numbers. By necessity, musicians have a better understanding of time because of the intricate meters and time signatures that keep a band or orchestra together.

The benefits aren't limited to the playing itself. When a child plays music, he learns to be on time for rehearsals. He also needs to plan his day and set aside time to practice his instrument. For better or for worse, a student sees the results of a lack of practice due to poor time management. Young musicians learn not only to keep time on their own but to keep time with others when playing in a group. All of the children with me at the ball game play music, and all are always on time both in class and for our extracurricular activities. It's not a coincidence. Whether you are able to give your child private lessons or make sure he plays in school, music must not be optional. Reading music is as important as reading itself.

Many schools today see it differently, and offer music only as an elective. This is a mistake. Music training should be required as part of a complete education. If your child reads music, plays music, and makes it a part of his daily existence, his life will be better for it. Through music, a student will learn to literally play with others, and without realizing it will develop time management skills that will be useful throughout the day, even when the instrument is not being played.

## All the World's a Stage

As with music, children who perform in plays have a much better understanding of time than those who do not. When I began directing plays with kids more than thirty years ago, I did not understand this at all. In my early years, creating a production with students was all about learning lines, blocking scenes, and sending an audience home happy.

With maturity, I observed that some children connected with audiences better than others, even though they were no louder, clearer, or more dynamic. It was all about their timing. When a child rehearses a play, and learns to recite lines and react to others, his sense of timing improves.

Consider this fantastic joke from Sir Ian McKellen. He tells it during his brilliant one-man show, *Acting Shakespeare.* Our class loves to do this joke onstage when performing various vignettes from Shakespeare. A couple of hours into the show, one of the kids will come out with a cup and say:

> You'll excuse me for having a drink when you're not allowed to have one. The human vocal system was not devised to be used for long periods without some lubrication. If you ever have a problem with your voice, don't talk. That's the quickest way to mend a broken voice. But if you have to speak, then you could do worse than try this homemade restorative, which is simply fresh-squeezed lemon juice with runny honey, poured in and stirred around until it's all dissolved and then you let it trickle over the back of the throat.
>
> [He takes a sip, and tells the audience, "It's good," which brings out soft giggles from the crowd. Then, after a long pause, comes the line that kills.]
>
> Actually, it's gin! [The crowd dies laughing.]
>
> [another dramatic pause]
>
> And the magic of the theater is, you will never know.

My students have told this joke onstage for years, to the delight of thousands of viewers. Better still; the kids have learned the importance of timing. If they do not pause before announcing that their medicine is merely booze, the crowd does not laugh nearly as much. They learn to say the final line *just* as the wave of laughter from the previous joke is dying down. If they wait until the room is silent, the joke falls flat. If they recite the line too soon, the previous laughter will drown out the final punch line.

When children perform music and theater, they discover that timing is everything. With guidance, it's not a big leap for them to grasp that this is true for all of life and not just the arts. Being in plays develops a child's speaking skills and the subtle gift of knowing not just what words to say but *when* to say them.

We want our children to have better lives than our own. If they value time, this dream becomes a more likely reality. Combine these books and films with ideas of your own. Pack a musical instrument and a script and then zip up your kid's backpack carefully. You won't want him to lose any of this priceless cargo.

## End of the First Inning

The first inning ended and the kids were happy and giggling as they compared score sheets. It hadn't been easy preparing these little ones for a night of baseball. I thought about Thornton Wilder, who was always interested in millions of stars, millions of people, and millions of souls. I contemplated the hundreds of hours these kids had spent learning about baseball, and it felt wonderful to see them having such a good time. And, like Wilder, I thought about those who came before.

I remembered Julia, one of the first kids I ever took to a ball game so many years ago. She was never a huge baseball fan. Gymnastics was her passion. Funnily enough, she was never even in my class. She had a different fifth-grade teacher, but she hung out in Room 56 as often as possible. She played music, acted in our Shakespeare plays, and was a shining star.

Just last month, I made the pilgrimage to Ithaca, New York, with my wife, Barbara, to visit Julia at Cornell. Little Julia, not so little anymore, was the first person in her family ever to make it to college, and she was attending a top Ivy League university. Given her humble beginnings, this would be considered a miracle by most.

She's a senior there now, majoring in chemical engineering. She has all sorts of job opportunities, internships, and graduate school offers being thrown her way. Her future is bright. That's not bad for a little girl who didn't speak English and whose father worked long hours anywhere he could to put food on the table. Whether he was taking orders in an eyeglass frame store or selling sandwiches at a mall, he always found ways to make sure his kid had a chance.

We had dinner with Julia at a little restaurant near the Cornell campus on a delightful spring evening. We laughed and even cried a bit thinking about the ten years we had known one another. Barbara talked about the old days, and inquired about kids we had lost contact with over the years. There were many who were just as wonderful and even brighter than Julia but were not graduating from college.

I'm always interested in learning from an exceptional young person the thinking behind her success. Julia mentioned to me that she had two roommates at Cornell. One had dropped out of school. The other had left campus for a while and had just recently climbed back in to work her way toward graduation. Only Julia was soaring to great heights. I asked her about her incredible success.

RAFE: What's the secret to all you've accomplished, Julia?

JULIA: (laughing) Fridays and Pomfret Castle. No question about it.

RAFE: (stumbling) Excuse me?

Julia explained to me that during high school she decided that Friday night was her favorite time of the week. Other students were relieved to have their classes finished and dropped everything to blow off steam. She had found the same to be true of her college classmates. But Julia approached things differently. Like her classmates, she loved to party. She was never much of a drinker, but guys and music and silliness were a big part of her life. Just not on Fridays. She told me that she studied particularly hard on Fridays, when she was still in her academic rhythm. It wasn't that she studied more hours than other students, it was *when* she hit the books that made a difference. She said that all our conversations about time had meant something to her. I had never even thought of the importance of Friday nights, but she had.

RAFE: So studying Hamlet helped. Remember Hamlet saying, "the readiness is all"?

JULIA: Of course. But to be honest, it meant much more to me when you took me to *Richard II* many years ago at the Oregon Shakespeare Festival.

RAFE: Really?

JULIA: I never, ever forgot act five, scene five. I even copied my favorite moment and pasted the quote above my desk. Before being murdered in Pomfret Castle, King Richard said, "I wasted time, and time doth now waste me." I wasn't going to ever let that be the epitaph on my grave.

Suddenly, I blinked and my mind was back at Dodger Stadium. I glanced to my right and the kids were getting ready for the second inning. I smiled and dreamed that they too, in time and with time, would grow up to be as special as Julia. I wasn't tired anymore.

# Keep Your Eye on the Ball

"Pay attention" might win the prize for the most frequently used phrase in a classroom. It would be a close contest with "listen up," "settle down," "quiet down," and, unfortunately, "shut up." Without question, the majority of teachers today complain that the most aggravating problem in their classrooms is that kids do not behave. They just don't listen.

This is a chapter about focus. Extraordinary students concentrate, and do so for very long periods of time. When reading a novel, these students do not begin by checking how many pages are in the book. They don't consider the length of a film printed on a DVD case before viewing the movie. And they listen incredibly well without being scared or threatened. When I travel with the kids, almost everywhere we go some kind stranger will approach me in an airport or a restaurant or a hotel lobby, and ask in wonder, "How in the world do you get those kids to listen with such purpose?"

These days, when it seems every restless child is automatically labeled as having Attention Deficit Hyperactivity Disorder (ADHD), people are impressed to see youngsters who can keep their eyes on the ball.

Of course, ADHD is a serious problem that does affect a small percentage of children in the world. These kids need expert help, and with the involvement of the right specialists and good parents, they can lead happy and productive lives.

But today, any kid who is looking out the window, not finishing assignments, or acting rude in class is diagnosed as suffering from this problem. Many children are being medicated when drugs are the last thing in the world that they need.

For most children, lack of focus is not a medical problem. They are often bored and unfortunately are living in a society that fuels their lack of concentration with countless distractions. This inability to focus can lead to disastrous results in the classroom as well as in life. Students who reach great heights have learned how not to be easily distracted. If a child can concentrate on school tasks, and, more important, on his own dreams and goals, his life will be better.

The second inning began and the Cardinals were coming up to bat. The stadium was still remarkably empty for a Friday night. My novice scorekeepers had discovered their observational rhythm. They grasped where to look on the various scoreboards to check for balls and strikes, and also knew how to confirm that the current hitter matched the corresponding line on their scorecard. They had not yet learned the complex series of statistics that more experienced baseball fans have already mastered: on-base percentages, earned-run averages, and slugging percentages. Nonetheless, they understood batting averages and statistics such as home runs and runs batted in. When hitters with batting averages above .300 walked to the plate, the children sat up a little straighter. The kids were doing a fine job.

And so were the Cardinals. The middle of their lineup aggressively went after the Dodgers' pitcher, and before you could say Stan Musial or Lou Brock, there were Cardinals on first and third with no one out. Even my beginning baseball pupils knew that falling far behind in the second inning would not be a good thing for their team. I pointed out that the Dodger infield was playing back, willing to sacrifice a run in hopes of turning a double play. The kids waited for the drama to unfold.

Suddenly, it was raining beach balls. This is an aggravating occurrence in many sports venues across the nation, but Dodger Stadium might be the worst offender. Fans take out beach balls, blow them up, and begin batting them around the crowd, often neglecting to consider the safety of those seated around them who might be focused on the game. Ye Rim, who was watching the field to see if the Dodgers were going to stop the Cardinals from scoring, got hit in the head. There were tears in her eyes— not from pain, but from the shock of getting hit in the head by a flying object, compounded by the discovery that people all around were laughing at her.

I touched her arm and explained. She was shaken and confused, and so were the other children. The kids watched the batter but had some questions for me.

JESSICA: What is all this?

RAFE:   Don't worry about it, Jessica. This happens quite a lot.

JESSICA: Why are these people doing this?

RAFE:  They think it's fun, I guess. It's entertaining for them.

JESSICA: But isn't the game supposed to be entertaining?

RAFE:  Yes, it is. But different people see things differently.

JIN UK: (who notices everything) What about the sign?

RAFE:  What sign?

JIN UK: When we entered the stadium, there was a big sign that said you could not bring in bottles, weapons, or beach balls. I read it twice.

RAFE:  Maybe they didn't see it.

For the kids, it was inconceivable that people attending a baseball game would ignore what was happening on the field to play with a ball in the stands, especially because doing so was against the posted rules of the stadium and could potentially injure unsuspecting fans. The conversation continued, with the kids pointing out that they are called *beach* balls because we use them at the *beach*, right? It was not easy to explain this kind of human behavior to a group of thoughtful ten-year-olds who were attempting to comprehend something that made no sense to them.

The situation deteriorated. The children noticed that the majority of the fans in our section were not watching the game at all. They had stood up and turned their backs to the field. Like rabbits, the number of beach balls had quickly multiplied, and now four of them were flying around our section. Fans were screaming and shrieking as balls flew from one row to another.

Hysterical laughter erupted when one ball hit an elderly woman in the head.

By this point, ushers had walked down the various aisles of the sections and were struggling to confiscate the balls. The attendants were mostly young people, probably in high school or college, trying to make a living. The crowd taunted and cursed at them as they sought to retrieve the brightly colored spheres.

About five rows in front of us, one of the balls rolled down the aisle and was picked up by a little boy who was with his father. The child was about five years old. A Dodger employee walked up the stairs and approached him. His father screamed, "Don't give it to her! Don't give it to her! Hit it! Hit it!" The boy obeyed his role model eagerly, and smacked the ball down several rows and away from the usher. The crowd roared its approval.

Finally, a solitary man grabbed the ball. As the crowd pressured the gentleman to hit it, he stood up and handed it to the usher. The two of them were then assaulted with howls of derision and foul language.

Meanwhile, there *was* a game going on, even if few people on the field level of section 12 at Dodger Stadium realized it. The Cardinals had scored on a spectacular play at home plate. With one out and men on first and third, the batter doubled, easily scoring the man from third. The runner on first was waved home, but a strong relay from the Dodger right fielder to the second baseman to the catcher made the play at home extremely close. The runner made a fabulous slide around the catcher, and barely touched the plate with his left hand as he flew home safely. The Cardinals led, 2–0. It is not an exaggeration to state that at least 90 percent of the fans in our section did not see any of this. They were too busy playing with their . . . well, you get the idea.

This is symptomatic of our times. It shouldn't come as a surprise that our kids do not focus in school when they live in a society that has forgotten how to pay attention. In this case, the kids even got to see a father *teach* his child not to pay attention. Is it any wonder that our schools are filled with children who can't or won't concentrate?

When the small child threw the ball away from the usher, it raised an interesting point: was he really behaving badly? After all, one man's "brat" is another man's "rascal." Many intelligent and good people have advanced the argument that this is a baseball game and fans who paid are allowed to do pretty much anything they want. Such reasoning ought to be rejected by thoughtful children. Young people need to learn that poor conduct even by the majority of fans doesn't make it right. The issue here is for children to develop a personal code of behavior, one that is strong enough to stand up to a mob mentality, whether of a sports crowd or elsewhere in life.

The assessment of behavior is a matter of opinion. But it is a fact that children in school today are not behaving or paying attention as well as they once did. Almost every veteran teacher has seen firsthand this decline in manners. The problem is compounded by devastation in the teaching ranks, as many fabulous professionals have thrown in the towel in discouragement at the increasing number of disruptive children. Serious students who want to pay attention and focus on lessons are often outnumbered by unruly classmates. In many cases, they are terrified to show passion and interest in their work, because such behavior often results in the same ridicule heaped on the man who gave the ball to the usher.

Children are better off when they develop and establish a personal code of behavior. I teach all children, including my own, Lawrence Kohlberg's six levels of moral development. Kohlberg's  simple hierarchy identifies six reasons people are motivated to behave in certain ways. At each successive level, the reason becomes more complex, and less tethered to a basic system of stimulus and response.

Level 1:  I do not want to get in trouble.
Level 2:  I want a reward.
Level 3:  I want to please someone.
Level 4:  I always follow the rules.
Level 5:  I am considerate of other people.
Level 6:  I have a personal code of behavior.

Children set off on the path to extraordinary when they dedicate themselves to reaching level 6 on Kohlberg's scale. Getting there is an ongoing process that requires patience and persistence. Do we refrain from stealing only because the police are near? Or do we not steal because we refuse to engage in that kind of behavior? Special children pay attention all the time; they understand that treating concentration as a part-time job won't help them achieve their goals. They focus at baseball games, and in school. We are kidding ourselves if we don't think there is a connection. Extraordinary children include the ability to focus as part of their personal code of conduct.

Ye Rim had started biting her lower lip. She's such an interesting little girl, a rare combination of deadly seriousness and water-balloon silliness. When she is troubled about something she bites her lower lip, and there are days when she leaves a bite mark on her beautiful face. The beach balls, the father, and the abusive fans had made her sad. I wanted to talk to her, but this was not the right moment.

She needed time and space to process what she had experienced. At a better time in the days ahead I might raise the issue. The Dodger organization had forbidden bringing beach balls into the stadium. Playing with them disturbs people who are trying to watch the game. It is disrespectful to the players, who give their all to win out on the field. It should be brought to the children's attention that this whole situation resulted because many people today have problems keeping their eyes on the ball, so to speak. Television and computer screens, cell phones, and other distractions have led to behavior—for instance, trying to pay for something while jabbering away on a cell phone—that has required a new set of newspeak terms to describe. It's sometimes called multitasking, but in many cases this is just a euphemism for being rude.

A pop fly to the shortstop and a groundout to second ended the top of the inning and the Cardinals were held to two runs. The kids were busy with their scorecards, tallying up the damage.

They may not have realized it, but scorekeeping was a way to increase their ability to concentrate on a single task. Yes, we were at a baseball game, but learning to keep statistics improves a child's ability to watch, listen, and record. In doing so, they were learning a skill that would serve them well whether they became a scientist or an artist. People mistakenly believe that these students perform well on standardized tests because they are more intelligent than other kids. That's not the case. They are able to attack each question with meticulous precision and analyze all the possible choices because they have learned to focus.

## Middle of the Second

With the Cardinals out and the teams switching sides, there was even more commotion in the stands as people arose to go to the restroom or get another hot dog. A young man of about nineteen or twenty saw the children writing down statistics.

YOUNG MAN: Hey, what are you guys doing?

AUSTIN:      Keeping score. It's fun.

YOUNG MAN: I heard about that. I've seen it too. Can you show me?

AUSTIN:      Sure, it's easy. Every position has a number.

YOUNG MAN: You mean every player has a number.

AUSTIN:      No, I mean position. The pitcher is 1, the catcher is 2, the first baseman is 3 . . .

[We need Abbott and Costello to begin "Who's on First?"]

YOUNG MAN: Ah, this is too complicated. I was hoping to show my little brother. He doesn't ever listen to me.

AUSTIN:      It's really not that hard. Just watch for a while. I'd be happy to show you.

YOUNG MAN: Naw, that's okay. See ya.

This was a nice guy. He was friendly to the kids and seemed to care about his little brother. Yet he was unwilling to spend even two minutes with Austin to learn something. Maybe he was really starving or just had to go to the bathroom, but his words suggested that he didn't think it was worth the effort.

Austin glanced over at me. We'd talked about this dozens of times. It takes energy to learn new things. It takes concentration and desire. As the Dodgers came up in the bottom of the second inning, the kids knew exactly who was batting next, what the score was, and what to expect. They were not baseball experts and certainly not geniuses. They simply had accepted the fact that paying attention and working to focus would make their lives better.

## Focus in a Backpack

If you don't want your child sitting in front of a computer with a remote control in one hand and an iPod in the other, you might consider putting some of the following tools in his backpack.

### Radio Days

Scoring baseball games is just a start, and you don't need to go to the stadium to do it. Your child can score at home, and for a real challenge have him score a game by listening to the radio. Since they cannot rely on sight, children improve their listening skills as they record what they hear. This is outstanding preparation for the art of taking notes in class. To add to the fun, organize a family activity reading Doris Kearns Goodwin's fascinating  book *Wait Till Next Year,* and learn how she and her father bonded as she scored Brooklyn Dodgers games as a child.

*Never Bored with Board Games*

Coach John Wooden of UCLA said, "Progress has always come from change, but change does not necessarily mean progress." Children today are mesmerized by computer and video games, but many experts believe they impair a child's ability to concentrate. High-profile, widespread advertising campaigns by clever companies try to convince buyers that these games are good for a child. Well, only in America. We're the country that ran ads years ago for Camel cigarettes boasting they were the favorite of doctors.

Television hypnotizes its viewers and dulls the response levels of children—they watch passively and do not have to concentrate. Computer screens are no better; a youngster who spends too much time glued to one does not develop the kind of long-term focus that a child needs to reach the greatest heights. When a kid loses in an electronic game, he merely starts again. This subtly reinforces the lesson that when he loses focus or screws up, he gets as many chances as he needs to make things right, a scenario that in no way resembles what will happen when he is taking exams or trying to survive in a difficult work situation.

There are outstanding games that, if played often, help a child focus and stay on task. They may not have flashing lights or bells and whistles, but they are absolutely fantastic in raising the bar when it comes to your child's powers of "stick-to-it-iveness."

Checkers, backgammon, and chess are great first steps on any child's journey into board games. There is no luck involved in winning and losing. The player not only contemplates his own moves but must consider the tactics of his opponent.

All these games have merit, but I'd like to cast my vote for chess. Learning to play chess well is a distinctive experience. Chess is a game like no other in its ability to teach a child to concentrate. If you are a parent and not a chess aficionado, you can't lose by starting your child with Brian Byfield's wonderful book *Every*  *Great Chess Player Was Once a Beginner.* It's simple and, better yet, a very funny read. It may seem surprising to connect laughter with chess, but Byfield's illustrations and explanations will have the reader giggling and learning at once. His colorful pictures include kindly old bishops with secretive twinkles in their eyes. Underneath their robes can be seen the bodies of the poor little pawns, which these saintly-looking old men have "murdered" during the game. The queens are savage war-riors that conjure up memories of *Alice in Wonderland.* The instructions have some of the funniest explanations of chess this side of a Charlie Chaplin film. The book is available from online retailers.

Once a child is hooked on the game, the next step is to find a chess club at school or in the community. Friendships can be formed with other kids who are walking their own path or attempting to break away from group-think. Sportsmanship, patience, and continued improvement at the game are all benefits waiting to be discovered by a young chess master.

For any family involved with chess, Steven Zaillian's 1993 film *Searching for Bobby Fischer* is a must-see. This underappreciated gem has been given a 100 percent approval rating on www. rottentomatoes.com, a Web site that aggregates film reviews from hundreds of different sources. The film is based on the true story of Josh Waitzkin, a child prodigy whose father learns that having his son be the best at anything isn't worth a penny if the cost of greatness is the boy's happiness. In this movie, chess comes alive on the screen. It's a great way to get your kid excited about the game and teach him a lesson about values at the same time.

Other games encourage different skills. Mastermind is a fantastic two-player logic game in which one player arranges a hidden sequence of four colored pegs while the other player attempts to break this "code" over a series of turns. This challenging board game was invented in 1970 by Mordecai Meirowitz, an Israeli postmaster and telecommunications expert. It is simple and has different levels of play, so it can be enjoyed by the very young and high school kids alike. The game can be learned in five minutes, but to play it well takes years of practice. As a child plays, his concentration will improve dramatically. The game is a first-rate guide to understanding math and logic concepts like combinations, permutations, and eventually even algorithms. Kids love playing it, and an occasional game with Mom or Dad will definitely strengthen brain muscles that need to be exercised regularly.

Scrabble, of course, should be a weekly adventure for all kids. In an era when writing and spelling proficiency has declined, this classic word game will improve your child's language skills. Regardless of the game's outcome, a child will have learned new words and strengthened his mental endurance. Show me a good Scrabble player, and I'll show you a confident reader, writer, and communicator.

### Models without Bikinis

With today's flood of complicated electronic games, it's easy to overlook the fact that simpler may in fact be better. Far fewer children today work on scale models at home or school. Yet, this activity can be highly beneficial to a child's development. Building models, whether of cars, boats, airplanes, or houses, teaches a child to read and follow directions carefully. Assembling a whole from the sum of hundreds of smaller parts inspires a child to explore the nature of the universe itself. Future engineers and chemists are born when children discover the joy of construction.

A more subtle result of a model-building project is an appreciation of history and of how our ancestors created this nation. When a child assembles a model of the *Mayflower* or Henry Ford's original Model T, he begins to value our history with far more profound understanding than can ever be learned in a workbook. As hobby shops are often difficult to find these days, it may be quicker to order good models online. Such sites as www.hobbylinc.com, www.revell.com, and www.ehobbies.com are just a few of the places where you'll find a wide range of models to fascinate a young builder. It's a wonderful way for kids to work together on a project and actually talk and listen to one another as they follow directions and create.

### The April Fool's Exam

This is not an original idea, and many teachers have probably run across it at some point in their career. For parents who are supporting their child's efforts in school or even offering homeschooling, the April Fool's exam is a fun way to teach students of any age the importance of paying attention and following directions. Teachers can also use this exam to great effect, as the laughs that come at the end will multiply when a group of students participates.

On April 1, remind your child that standardized tests will be administered soon, and tell them you have a little exercise to help them prepare. Act easygoing and calm as you assure them that this little exam is just for fun. As this is preparation for the real tests your child will be taking soon, tell him to follow instructions, not to talk during the test, and to remain silent when finished until you collect and grade the paper.

Here's the joke: it's a trick test. Type about five lines of directions, single-spaced, and below add a series of numbered questions. Most kids will eagerly skip the directions and immediately begin the first question. The instructions should read something like this:

> This is a test to see how well you can follow directions. Work quickly, as you will have only fifteen minutes to finish. Be sure you read every question on the test before beginning. When you have finished all twenty-five questions, you may put your pencil down and read a book. Good luck and remember to try your very best.

Lots of children will not notice the third sentence, which tells them to read the *entire* exam before beginning.

1. Write your first and last names. _____
2. In what state do you live? _____
3. What is your birthday? _____

So far so good. Students often simply begin filling in the first question, as the form seems so obvious. By question 4, see if the kids will follow directions no matter how silly things seem.

4. Take your right shoe off and place it on your desk.
5. Stand up, face the east, and say out loud, "I love King Kong and Godzilla."
6. How many brothers and sisters do you have?_____

It's amazing how many students, particularly if you set things up correctly, will do the most outrageous things if asked. Design the test with a few or even more than a few outrageous requests. Always, though, keep the kids guessing by interspersing mundane questions. The fun comes with the last question:

25. Do not do ANY of the first twenty-four questions. Simply leave your paper blank, put your pencil down, remain silent, and discover if you have made an April Fool of yourself!

Your child will eventually laugh at himself, realizing that had the instructions been followed carefully, the entire situation could have been avoided. If this test is designed in good fun, no one ends up with hurt feelings and a valuable lesson is learned. Those who do not fall for the joke have had their focus validated, so, April Fool or not, everyone wins.

### Literature for an Alert Mind

Charles Dudley Warner, the American essayist and novelist, wrote that "nothing is worth reading that does not require an alert mind." A child who reads for pleasure is going to concentrate with more passion and endurance than the majority of children, who read only required assignments. It's inspiring to see how many families have started book clubs. Mary Alden in Pasadena, who has two wonderful daughters, Katie and Annie, started a book society years ago that involved several families reading together. They select first-rate literature, read the books, and then gather for a weekly discussion.

In these family clubs, books are not being read for school assignments or to pad a résumé. Reading is simply an enriching pastime. It might sound unnecessary to carve out separate time for reading, but these days it's more essential than ever. Shockingly, more than a few school districts have practically outlawed reading for pleasure. Particularly at the elementary level, schools sign contracts with publishers to use a basal reader to teach reading. Part of the contract is that other reading sources must be removed from the classroom. All across the nation, I have met sensational but frustrated teachers who have had "literacy coaches" come into their rooms and instruct class leaders to follow the script of a basal reader. Many teachers actually have to read outstanding works with their classes in secret to avoid being reprimanded for not using some banal, district-selected text.

Parents who want more for their kids have to take matters into their own capable hands. Reading for pleasure helps students excel in many pursuits, from art projects to scientific experiments. Reading for extended periods of time and then discussing the content with peers is a priceless exercise in focus.

For elementary-school children, mysteries are particularly enjoyable and stimulating. The reader has to mine the text carefully for clues because a puzzle needs to be solved. A brilliant mystery to consider is Ellen Raskin's Newbery Medal–winning book, The Westing Game. The novel is filled with deception and humor, as a brilliant but bratty teenage protagonist named Turtle Wexler tries to solve a murder mystery as part of a quest to inherit $200 million. She has to focus to solve the puzzle, and your child will be in Turtle's shoes every step of the way.

Let's make sure all teenagers read J. D. Salinger's masterpiece, *The Catcher in the Rye.* In chapter 10, there is a terribly funny and yet sad moment when Holden Caulfield sits in a depressing night-club ("the band was putrid") and dances with a group of out-of-town girls that he dubs "the three witches." As Holden dances with the most attractive of the three, he tries to start a conversation with her, but she is straining her neck in the hope of seeing a movie star. Every time Holden says something her response is "What?" It's bit-terly funny. Finally, Holden sarcastically tells her that she is a won-derful conversationalist. "Whadga say?" she replies. It's great fun to read this with young people and listen to them chuckle in amusement. They laugh not only at Holden but at themselves, be-cause every kid has experienced the frustration of trying to have a conversation with a friend who is lost in the world of his iPod. "What?" is an all-too-familiar response in schools where so many children have forgotten or never learned how to pay attention.

The inscription over the door at the library at Thebes states, "Medicine for the Soul." Literature needs to be a joyous and daily part of a child's life. When getting together for a book club or read-ing with your child at night, never forget the words usually attrib-uted to Mark Twain: "The man who does not read good books has no advantage over the man who can't read them."

## Join Together with the Band

When asked by concerned parents what they can do to help their child learn to pay better attention, I always give the same piece of advice: get your kid a library card and a musical instrument. The payoffs for any young musician are infinite, but for the purpose of this discussion let's stick to the subject of focus.

When a child practices an instrument, he gets something rarely found in other lessons—immediate feedback. He hears a melody in his head; his brain knows the sound he is trying to create. When a note is played incorrectly the musician can hear the mistake instantly. This is not the case with most tasks. Students often complete numerous math problems incorrectly, repeating the same mistakes (sometimes even committing them to memory) before a teacher or parent catches the error and takes the time to undo the damage. With music, however, a child can understand that a misstep has been made even if an adult is not around to point it out. This instant notification in the ear motivates the player to concentrate and do it again until it sounds right.

Practicing along with a CD improves timing and intonation. Beginning guitarists in my class learn the second movement of Antonio Vivaldi's gorgeous Concerto in D. Each musician gets a copy not only of the sheet music but of a CD recording of the piece performed by a professional. Playing each night along with an expert while marshaling the level of concentration normally employed by a surgeon, the beginner soon sounds like a professional himself.

An added bonus is that once a student becomes competent, he still must learn to work with others. Young musicians discover that everyone might be playing the same piece, and yet timing and tone vary from performer to performer. A song that sounds fantastic in a child's bedroom might not sound as good when twelve kids play it together. They must look at one another and

listen until each child is in the heart and mind of his fellow musicians. When the focus becomes so strong that twelve sound like
one, the beauty of the music and the happiness of the children
are remarkable.

## The Art of the Matter

Wise parents and counselors encourage young people to do what
they love. It's good when kids have big dreams, but without laser-
like attention to details, those dreams rarely materialize. A paint-
brush or sketch pad may be the right tool to help a child achieve
that higher level of focus. Such disciplined training can begin at
the local museum's Saturday art session or during a third-period
class in high school. If a youngster is immersed in the arts, the
rewards will continue to come years after a painting is hung. It's
just one more activity that will create an opportunity for a young
person to grasp the fundamental importance of staying on task.
But it is only an opportunity. Art can open doors, but it is still
the student who must walk through.

Joanna was a high schooler who loved trying new things, and
so she signed up for a ceramics class. From her first touch of the
clay, Joanna found true love. She had always been a top scholar
in a wide variety of subjects, and had a particular fascination
with French. Yet her introduction to pottery awakened her passion. Despite having no interest in making art her career, she
knew instantly that she would be a potter for life.

She made an arrangement with the janitor of the school that
allowed her to work late into the evening, some nights even past
eleven o'clock. There was too much noise, she explained, during

school hours. Other kids blasted music or talked to their friends as they worked. Joanna desired quiet. She hated distractions. Though she was by nature a gregarious young lady and practically effervescent with her friends, she wanted only silence when she created her art. And as days turned into weeks and weeks into months, Joanna developed real talent. Her works won her attention and awards.

Later that year, her school chose its ten best artists to be featured in a show displaying these budding Hamadas' inspiring creations. All of these talented young people had made beautiful pieces. All had sacrificed and worked hard. But none had Joanna's focus, and this made all the difference. Her creations were jaw-droppingly good; they looked like art you would buy at the gift shop of the Metropolitan Museum of Art in New York City.

It was a magnificent exhibition, but you had to feel a little sorry for the other nine artists. The entire crowd was gathered around Joanna's pieces. Their eyes were glued to her extraordinary work. Her focus had called forth theirs.

But don't let Joanna's dedication make you think of her as some sort of robotic automaton devoted slavishly to work. She was and is a true kook. Joanna didn't like getting up for school in the morning, so she would sleep in her school uniform at night: this way she could climb out of bed and go straight to class. She played outlandish practical jokes on people. But as a child, she also played chess and Scrabble and built models. The clarinet was her primary instrument, but she dabbled in guitar as well. She carried all these things in her backpack for years, and the sum of those hours she spent concentrating was the powerful focus that allowed her to create extraordinary works of art.

Today she attends Brown University. She spent one summer studying in France, where her mornings included cooking with French families, her afternoons drinking lots of wine, and her spare time seeing as much of the country as possible. But if she spent her days roaming, at night she was easy to find: tucked away in a small studio in Lyon where she sat in front of a pottery wheel and continued to make the world more beautiful.

## End of the Second

The Dodgers did not score, which was bad for Dodger fans but good for beginning scorekeepers. With most of the players not reaching base, it was easy to keep track of the inning. A quick glance at the kids revealed that they were having a terrific time, but Ye Rim was still biting her lip. Shut up, I told myself. Leave her alone. She could figure things out for herself, and not everything had to be accomplished that night.

Suddenly she asked me if she could leave her seat during the break between innings, walk down the aisle, and take a picture of the field. She reached into her little pack and took out a small camera I did not know she had brought with her.

YE RIM: I'm just going down there. Back in a second. Jessica, come with me.

RAFE:   Ye Rim! This is cool! When did you become a photographer?

YE RIM: I went to the library last week and found this book I like a lot. It told me all sorts of tips for taking good pictures. I haven't learned them all yet, but they said there's one rule a good photographer always remembers. I want to try it out.

RAFE:        Okay. Be careful, you two.

I kept an eye on them as they walked down the aisle. Fortunately the stadium was still quite empty, so it was easy for them to negotiate the steps. I saw Ye Rim and Jessica snap a few pictures before they returned to their seats. Best of all, Ye Rim wasn't biting her lip anymore.

I had to ask her a question.

RAFE:        Ye Rim?

YE RIM:    Yes? [getting ready to score the third inning]

RAFE:        What was the photography rule you were talking about? The first rule?

YE RIM:    Rule number one: *Get closer.*

As is so often the case, I was wrong. I thought the beach ball incident had deflated this little girl's spirit, and I had been mentally planning a pep talk for her in the days to come. I needn't have worried. Ye Rim had added to the "code that she would live by." In getting closer with her focus, she had the vision to ignore beach balls and other unnecessary distractions.

# I Can See for Miles and Miles

The third inning was about to begin. The Cardinals were going to try to add to their lead. The sun had set, but it remained a very pleasant summer evening in Los Angeles. The children were quite comfortable in their T-shirts.

During the break, the majority of the fans had been fixated on the gigantic Diamond Vision screen over left field showing a continuous stream of television commercials with the volume turned up full blast.

In the classic 1962 film *The Manchurian Candidate*, staff sergeant Raymond Shaw makes a powerful observation, one that should be shared constantly with every child who wishes to go beyond the ordinary: "Have you noticed that the human race is divided into two distinct, irreconcilable groups? Those who walk into rooms and automatically turn television sets on, and those who walk into rooms and automatically turn them off."

Parents, television is killing your child's potential.

This may seem obvious, oversimplified, and blunt. Well, as

the Stage Manager in *Our Town* warns the audience when the graveyard's dead begin speaking, "Some of the things they'll say might hurt your feelings, but that's the way it is." Everyone seems to know that children should not be spending enormous amounts of time in front of screens, but the fact is, they are, and not enough is being done to stop the development of a behavior pattern that is fatal to a child's potential.

As the Cardinals were batting in the top of the third, a group of fans arrived to take the seats in the previously empty row in front of us. It was tough to miss them. They were late to the game, and upon reaching their seats they continued to stand and have a discussion about who should sit where. In many baseball stadiums, such as Petco Park in San Diego and Minute Maid Park in Houston, there is a thoughtful policy where ushers at the entrances to aisles politely ask fans not to take seats when a batter is up. People are asked to wait to be seated between batters as a courtesy to other fans. It would be nice if such a policy was enforced by the spectators themselves, but because such blanket consideration would be asking the impossible, many stadiums take the time to remind people to think of others. But when this game was being played, Dodger Stadium had no such policy; consequently Cesar, Austin, and their friends watched the scoreboard to keep track of what was going on because their view was blocked by the new neighbors, who remained standing for several minutes.

The latecomers consisted of four men, probably in their late twenties or early thirties, and a child who was about four or five. The child had an electronic game with him and was given the aisle seat. Head down and furiously pushing buttons, he was completely oblivious to all that was going on around him. This young tot would not have known the difference between a base-ball game and a trip to the zoo. The little screen was all that mattered. Cesar looked at him and shot me a glance, his eye-brows raised. Cesar was being raised by parents who had strict rules about screen time in their home, and he understood why his parents were so firm. He had trouble comprehending why other parents allowed screens to become the dominant force in their children's lives.

Searching the Internet will produce a plethora of articles from children's health magazines all over the world relating to this problem. The statistics might vary slightly from country to country and magazine to magazine, but the results boil down to the same thing: too much television is bad for all of us, and for young people in particular.

According to most experts, kids spend about seven hours a day watching television or looking at a computer screen. Research has discovered that 70 percent of kids today have a television in their bedroom and that these kids score between seven to nine points lower on standardized language and math tests than children who do not. There is also a direct correlation between increased television viewing and the decreasing percentage of kids who graduate from college. The frightening statistics march on. More than half of American homes have a television on even when no one is watching! This research has also concluded that television's damaging effects cut across socioeconomic lines, meaning that children from wealthy families suffer just as much as children who are poor. Television is an equal opportunity denier.

It is true that there are quality programs on television. The His-tory Channel is incredibly informative. Cooking channels, docu-mentaries, and first-rate dramas can be beautifully produced.

And sometimes people will find an outstanding educational show for preschoolers and cite evidence that kids who watch this particular show do better in the primary grades.

But most television programming does not encourage active participation or close watching. For every great documentary that can open a child's eyes to new ideas, there are fifteen to twenty reality shows, trashy dramas, or celebrity news magazine shows that demand little more than tuning in and dropping out. And let's not get started on the commercials. Leaving little ones to make distinctions on their own about which programs are useful and which waste their time is a recipe for disaster. Given the odds, it's far more likely that your kid will end up watching trash than watching treasure.

Despite the few good things on television, then, the fact is that children spend almost seven hours a day involved in an activity that is dangerously unhealthy for their development. The problem becomes figuring out how to stop this pattern. It is one of the most difficult tasks in raising a child. Television's power is scary. There are children today who cannot identify the president but can sing thirty jingles for products that have been advertised on TV before their hypnotized eyes. Big Brother is not only watching, but filling young minds.

Anyone raising a child has witnessed the destructive potential of the screen. I regularly take a group of students to the Shakespeare Festival in Ashland, Oregon. It's a fabulous place for kids to attend plays, learn about the theater, and have a wonderful time. Normally about fifty Hobart Shakespeareans study for a year to earn the privilege to attend this celebration. They stay in Ashland for ten days, mixing theater with swimming, reading, and playing soccer. One afternoon during a particular trip, many of the students were scheduled to watch *Othello* while others had some free time. Some participated in a furiously contested soccer game played in the local park. Others cooled off in the pool and read *Alice in Wonderland* while getting a suntan. A boy named Michael decided to stay in and watch television in his hotel room.

Later, the students attended a regular nightly meeting to discuss the day's events before going to bed. Over milk and cookies, the kids debated the merits of *Othello*. Most thought it was an outstanding production. A few were not happy with Desdemona's performance but liked the play nonetheless. The soccer players told hilarious stories about their day, and several of the girls giggled over a lifeguard at the pool with whom they had fallen in love. When I heard that Michael had chosen to watch three hours of television, I asked him what he had seen. He didn't know. He could not name one program or even describe what he had viewed. It was frustrating for him and heartbreaking to see.

Having taught thousands of students in more than a quarter of a century, I have witnessed certain patterns in classroom performance. One constant is that in every class there are students who underachieve. These are good kids who come to school and are not especially disruptive or mean, but their scholarship is mediocre. They get 70 percent right on math tests when peers who are no smarter get everything right, and this pattern occurs across all subjects. In almost every case, these underachievers are the same children who spend many hours watching television or playing computer games. Screens have become the common denominator for a child's failure to reach his considerable potential.

In studying Shakespeare, I have heard several experts define tragedy as not something that is merely bad, but something that is bad that should have been good. We weep when Hamlet dies because he is such a wonderful prince and could have made a magnificent king, the rose of the fair state. It is not an overstatement to label the destructive power of television as tragic. These mind-numbing results explain why concerned parents and teachers have desperately and understandably tried anything and everything to prevent kids from falling prey to the lure of screens.

One such teacher I know was a dedicated young man who worked in the projects of an inner city. He was everything a teacher should be: bright, passionate, caring, and eager to make a difference. One year, he noticed that one of his fifth-grade students never did any homework. Morning after morning, when assignments were collected, this bleary-eyed young lady would mumble that her work was not completed.

The teacher finally decided that enough was enough. Phone calls and letters home had not produced any improvement. One evening at six o'clock, he knocked on the door of the family's apartment. When the mother opened the door, the teacher was not surprised to find the child sitting in front of a television set with a plate of food in hand, shoveling in every morsel without taking her eyes off the screen.

The teacher explained to the mother that her daughter was falling behind and that her schoolwork had to improve. The mother responded that this ten-year-old child watched television every night until almost two A.M.! Before the teacher could even express shock, the mother threw up her hands in surrender and said, "What can I do?"

The teacher told her all the right things. As the parent she had the power to turn off the television. At the very least, she could make sure her child had finished her homework before watching. The mother promised she would do this, but after two more days of no homework, the teacher was knocking on the door again.

He reminded the mother of her promise, but once again was given the answer that "there was nothing she could do."

"Well," said the dedicated teacher, "there's something I can do." And with that, he took their television!

No kidding, he picked it up and walked out of the house.

For those who are working diligently with kids, you've got to love the passion and the sentiment behind this outrageous act. In many ways one wants to commend this teacher for original thinking. But after the laughter stops, we need to dig a bit deeper. This teacher's behavior is understandable, but it is not good teaching. In fact, it's not teaching—it's bullying.

The ultimate goal in raising a child is to get him to *turn off his own television set*. We can take the cigarette or bottle away from the addict, but that is not the cure. And besides, we cannot simply remove the danger of television. It's there and it's a reality. The real challenge is to teach a child the reason *why* television can rob him of his potential and get him to make his own decision. As with all the skills discussed in this book, this takes time. For all we've said about the special skills a child puts in his backpack, this is the one time that what's important is not what he puts *in* but what he leaves *out*. A child who chooses to limit his time in front of a screen enormously increases his chances of finding an avenue to greatness.

## Middle of the Third

The Cardinals added a run in the top of the inning and led, 3–0. As is the normal state of affairs at sports stadiums, the instant the half-inning was over the crowd was assaulted with music and televised images from the giant screen in the outfield. Practically no one was having a conversation. The sound was being blasted at such a high volume that it was impossible to hear anything. The young students were working on their score sheets and making sure the Cardinal who had knocked in the run was given proper credit for an RBI.

Among the kids, Cesar was the biggest baseball fan. He followed the Dodgers and played on an organized team three times a week. This young man had been a leading participator in class discussions regarding television. He once complained in exasperation, "Why play video baseball when you can play *baseball*?"

If you are at a ball game with your child, know that there are teachable moments between innings when parents can work to instill in their children what it takes to avoid screens. During this particular break the screen flashed a game in which the crowd would try to guess under which of three shells a baseball was hiding, a takeoff on the old carnival trick. Clever graphics and bright colors had the people oohing and aahing. Cesar shot me his trademark grin and kept to his tabulation of baseball statistics.

Telling children to turn off the boob tube "because I said so" will not be any more effective than just telling them to say no to drugs. The solution is more complicated than that. It involves a constant and gentle-but-firm series of discussions. The consistent suggestion that television should not dominate one's life will plant the seed to help kids turn off the television on their own. By modeling this behavior, parents can encourage the seed to germinate.

Occasionally a lucky strike that drives home this message is thrown right down the middle of the plate. In October 2007 the students in Room 56 were watching a Red Sox playoff game when the camera caught Sox fan and award-winning author Stephen King reading during a break between innings. When asked by a reporter why he was doing that, King answered that he could usually read eighteen pages during the game, but with Fox doing the broadcast, their longer commercials gave him time for twenty-seven! It was a wonderful thing for kids to see. Those of us trying to fight against screens need all the help we can get.

## Bottom of the Third

The bottom of the inning began. The tiny child in front of us continued to play with his electronic game while each of the four men with him drank a second beer. The students with me had done a good job of handling the barrage of commercials and nonsense being force-fed to them between innings for the last hour.

Learning how to discriminate between what to watch and when to watch is an essential skill for a child to master, and it is a talent that can be learned at any time or place. Classes may end at three P.M., but learning must never stop. The students at the game with me did not decide to take control of their viewing habits in three easy steps. Rather, their wise behavior was the result of a slow, steady succession of thoughtful lessons.

It's amusing to point out how many television screens are in places where they don't need to be. Televisions are at sporting events, in restaurants, and even in cars. Monitors are now forced on people in line at the supermarket or at the gas station filling their tanks. It would be funny if it were not so frightening. Jessica and Ye Rim once told the class that they saw television screens in the bathroom of a restaurant. They could barely contain their laughter as they giggled, "Who watches TV on a toilet?"

The previous fall, the kids at the game and twenty-five of their classmates had taken a trip to Washington, D.C. Beforehand, the children had earnestly studied the Constitution, United States history, and the memorials and monuments they would visit. But history was only part of the excursion's focus. Equal time was given to learning and practicing life skills. Preparation included packing suitcases, checking into hotels, and, of course, limiting screen time. Watching television defeats the purpose of travel and field trips, which is to explore new adventures and sights specific to the destination. Watching television can be done anywhere.

Before getting on the plane to Washington, the kids had a fascinating experience. After surprising the ticket agents with their organization and preparedness at getting their bags tagged and put through the X-ray machine, the children queued up to go through security. Upon seeing a long line of youngsters, a TSA worker spoke up. His questions were a bit irritating to the children but understandable when one considered the endless rush of disorganized and rude school groups with which this gentleman was used to dealing.

TSA:  Quiet down! [The kids weren't talking.] Place your backpacks and shoes on the belt. Take your cell phones and Game Boys out of your pockets.

KIDS:  We don't have Game Boys.

TSA:  Don't play with me. We'll find them.

KIDS:  We really don't have them.

(They began to go through the security scanner.)

TSA:  (checking a boarding pass)  You're going to Washington, D.C.?

KIDS:  Yes, we are.

TSA:  That's a long flight. Too bad your teacher doesn't let you bring Game Boys.

KIDS:  We can bring them if we want to. We just don't.

TSA:  (confused) I don't get it.

KIDS:  Have a nice day, sir.

The kids noticed that adults put the screen pressure on them. People treated them as "strange" when they were not like the little boy with the electronic toy at the baseball game. The coercion to conform continued after we entered the aircraft. Spotting the group of kids, a rather worried stewardess approached me.

FLIGHT ATTENDANT: How many do you have?

RAFE:  A total of thirty-three with the two adults.

FLIGHT ATTENDANT: (concerned) Well, we can give all of your children DVD players.

RAFE:                        Why would you do that? [The kids
                             are watching and listening.]

FLIGHT ATTENDANT: To give them something to do.

RAFE:                        No, thank you. They have some-
                             thing to do.

FLIGHT ATTENDANT: The flight is almost five hours
                             long.

RAFE:                        They have books. They're going to
                             read.

FLIGHT ATTENDANT: You can do that?

It's not the flight attendant's fault. She is part of a vicious cir-
cle that encourages her to pass out DVD players. Children today
often do not behave themselves, and this problem gets exacer-
bated on a long plane ride. Pastimes such as reading or working
on a crossword puzzle have come to be considered obsolete by
many people, so flight attendants are left with little recourse but
to perpetuate the act of throwing screens at children. It was good
for the students to see this. It's important for them to observe the
forces that lead many children to watch screens seven hours
a day.

As the flight began its descent into Washington, D.C., the
children were exposed to something they found even more frightening. The announcement was made over the loudspeakers that all
portable electronics had to be turned off. Headphones were removed and laptops stored away. However, the video screens were
showing the *Late Show with David Letterman,* and the witty host
was interviewing a celebrity. Although no one had headphones on
and there was no sound, the majority of people *continued to watch*

*the screen* even though it was impossible to know what was being said. They watched a talk show with absolutely no understanding of what was going on. Examples like this remind a youngster that his path away from screens is the healthier one.

## The Bigger Picture

It's fun to observe young people who have passed "Television 101" move on to more advanced thinking. Later that week in Washington, D.C., some of the kids asked if they could catch up on the news. They turned on CNN one evening to find out what was going on in the world. As if to hammer home the point about screens, the lead story was about some adults who got into a fight in front of an electronics store as they jockeyed for position to buy the latest video game system. This led to all sorts of wise observations on the part of the children.

The obvious point was the sheer lunacy of adults becoming violent in pursuit of Christmas gifts. The brilliant deduction, however, was when some of the kids began to wonder who had the power to make this the most important story of the day. On this same day the United States was at war in Iraq, with soldiers fighting and dying, and thousands were perishing of AIDS in Africa. The students had discovered a frightening truth. Television not only wastes one's time but subtly shapes our values. It is this subliminal seduction that trains minds to believe that athletes are more important than global warming, or that a fight over gaming systems is more important than news of significant international consequence.

Through constant exposure and discussion, these young people were hip to the danger of these influences. No one will ever have to take away their television sets. They have the knowledge and capacity to monitor themselves.

And for a laugh, make sure children remember the words of Groucho Marx: "I find television to be very educating. Every time somebody turns on the set, I go in the other room and read a book."

## Keeping Television Out of the Backpack

Raising a child strong enough to resist the omnipresence of the tube is a nonstop battle. Good parenting skills, including role modeling and dinner-table conversations with the television turned off, are the key to helping a child remain free from the clutches of Big Brother. Here are a few specific things you can do to keep your child from falling prey to the temptations of television.

### Set Reasonable Limits (No Barbed Wire or Handcuffs Necessary)

A child needs help to resist the spellbinding power of a television set. Setting consistent limits is necessary to help a young person build a life that does not center on a screen. The American Academy of Pediatrics offers several suggestions for parents:

- Set a time limit for your child's viewing.
- Do not allow television on school nights even if homework is finished.

- Be consistent with the media plan. Do not change rules. Nothing on television could be so important as to warrant altering the house policy.
- Schedule television viewing in advance. Do not allow your child to watch indiscriminately and channel surf.
- Keep television, video, and computer games out of the bedroom.
- Television is best approached as a family activity. Watch something worthwhile together and discuss the program when it is over. Encourage kids to ask questions and draw conclusions about what they have seen and to evaluate its message.

*Literature to the Rescue, and You Are Captain Nathan*

For those raising small children, *The Wretched Stone* by Chris Van Allsburg is a brilliant tale that can help children see the danger of television. Van Allsburg is perhaps known best for his masterpiece, *The Polar Express,* but *The Wretched Stone* is just as important. This clever tale is told as a series of entries from a ship's log. A crew of sailors discovers a mysterious, glowing stone on an island. They are so fascinated by the stone that they bring it aboard and do nothing all day but stare at its mesmerizing glow. The men neglect their chores and the ship begins to deteriorate rapidly. The crew loses all ambition and eventually they turn into apes. Due to their negligence, the ship and its crew are almost destroyed by a storm. But the head of the ship, Captain Nathan, rescues the men by inspiring them to return to their glory days of reading and playing music. Small children love the

B/M

fantastic symbolism of the men turning into apes, a development that doesn't seem like too much of an exaggeration once kids have grasped the dangers of television. Beautiful illustrations will entertain young readers and encourage them to heed Van Allsburg's warning. And parents will be reminded that all children need a Captain Nathan to help steer their ship safely.

A perfect book to help older children become more discerning about what they watch is George Orwell's funny yet tragic novel *Animal Farm*. Whether you read it with a fifth grader as an allegory about the abuse of power or delve into its Russian history context with high school students, this brilliant work of satire looks at mind control as only Orwell could. By studying the character of Squealer, the propagandist pig who "can turn black into white," a student will learn to think twice before accepting information as true without giving it serious thought. The lessons of *Animal Farm,* once read and digested, are never forgotten, which is great for a child and bad news for forces that want him to stop thinking for himself.

During a book club or family reading hour, be sure that middle and high school students read Ray Bradbury's exquisite *Fahrenheit 451.* In Bradbury's nightmarish vision of the future, firemen do not douse fires but start them: it is their job to burn libraries. The book's protagonist, Guy Montag, is a fireman who becomes self-aware and begins to question his destructive behavior. People often read this classic as an outcry against censorship, but Bradbury himself stated that above all, the story is about the menace of television. The people of the society described in *Fahrenheit 451* do not think or question. Instead, they spend their days and nights watching "parlor walls," which entertain and mesmerize them, allowing the government to control them. The power of these screens is so strong that Montag's wife is unhappy having only three of them in her room. She desperately wants a fourth so she can be completely surrounded. Every evening people stare fixedly at their screens watching the government chase and kill enemies of the state. It requires only a small leap of imagination to make the chilling connection between the people riveted by chases in *Fahrenheit 451* and the wall-to-wall coverage of chases on cable news today. It's downright brilliant and shocking enough to jolt young people out of their submission to their own "parlor walls."

## Reel Time

Two films are excellent choices to help guide middle and high school students to see television for what it is. Sidney Lumet's 1976 classic *Network* features an Academy Award–winning script from Paddy Chayefsky. Although the film is more than twenty-five years old, its brutally satiric edge may be even more on point today than when the film initially landed in theaters. *Network* shocked the public by showing television producers who care only about ratings and earnings. Talk about foreshadowing! In this movie, even terrorists negotiate with producers for their fifteen minutes of fame and are given prime-time exposure. *Network* (a film for only mature high school students guided by wise adults), forces the viewer to consider the absurdity of supporting an institution that encourages this kind of behavior, and will inspire young minds to reject the popularity of current TV shows that espouse similar values.

⓪ Better still to watch in the quest to educate students is Robert Redford's outstanding 1994 production *Quiz Show*. Based on Richard Goodwin's account of the game show scandals of the 1950s, this true story is filled with believable and basically good people who succumb to the tantalizing enticements offered by the chance to be on television. Before viewing the film, have your young thinker commit its promotional tagline to memory: "Fifty million people watched, but nobody saw a thing."

Extraordinary young people are not necessarily brighter than their peers; they have merely developed sharper vision and see the picture more clearly.


## End of the Third

Fortunately, some kids refuse to be dumbed down by screens, and Cesar is a perfect example. He was excited because his Dodgers had actually pushed across a run and had tightened the score to 3–1. Cesar practically never watches television. He has found better things to do, because his parents taught him to be aware of the dangers television watching can pose. The screen has little place in their pursuit of the American Dream. Cesar does not watch for many reasons, but the most important one is the example set by his older sister, Tracy.

It bears repeating: extraordinary children reach great heights over a period of many years rather than in an instant. I first met Tracy six years earlier when she was a fifth grader. She was a beautiful and bright young lady, eager to do her work correctly, and happy to participate in class discussions. Tracy was intelligent and hardworking, but so were many others in her class.

Still, she was one of the two brightest stars. Though others could calculate faster, jump higher, or write more creatively, there was never a doubt that in the years to come, Tracy would go on to do special things.

It came to pass. Tracy won a huge scholarship to an elite private high school known for producing some of our nation's top scholars. And from this cream-of-the-crop preparatory school, where kids arrived in limousines and spent their days with private tutors, school counselors and teachers called me often to praise Tracy. She was different, they gushed. Gifted. Special. Unique. Extraordinary.

A high school senior today, Tracy has the enviable problem of being solicited by almost every top university in the nation. Plane tickets have been sent to woo her to various campuses, and exciting internships are being pitched to her.

Recently, she spent a day in Room 56, a heroine returning to the forever leaky classroom, where she happily sat answering questions from my current students. Surrounded by awestruck kids hoping to one day be in her shoes, Tracy offered the young admirers the usual list of advice: read, study hard, take school seriously, ask lots of questions, choose your friends carefully, and find a balance between work and play. One student asked, "What's the most important advice you can give us?"

"That's an easy one," Tracy replied quickly. "Stay away from television. It weakens and limits you."

She asked if the kids had watched *Quiz Show* yet, and upon finding they had not, gave them a short summary of the film. Dishonest television producers had lied to Congress and completely avoided responsibility for defrauding the American people. Congressional investigator Dick Goodwin, played by Rob

Morrow, makes a sad remark that Tracy never forgot. Goodwin says, "I thought we were gonna get television . . . but the truth is, television is going to get us."

"Don't let that happen to you," Tracy warned the little ones. As they took this in, the silence in the room was deafening.

# Crossroads

It's not overly dramatic to use the word *crucial* in emphasizing the importance of teaching children about smart decision making. Even if a youngster makes good use of time, has focus, and avoids television, poor choices can instantly take away all the outstanding prospects those other fine qualities afford him.

It has nothing to do with intelligence. President Clinton is a perfect example, and one I often use in class discussions. Clearly, the man who still believes in a place called Hope is a very smart individual; despite this, he made a terrible decision to become sexually involved with a White House intern. I do not say this to be self-righteous. We are all human, we all make mistakes, and none of us would look good if held under the presidential microscope. I am not a close personal friend of Bill Clinton, but I am quite sure that he would do anything to go back in time and make a different decision if given the chance.

To help children develop a code of conduct, they need to be shown that even extraordinary people can make terrible decisions.

For this reason young ones should be schooled in the art of choosing the right path when faced with a crossroads.

It was past nine P.M. when the fourth inning began. The stadium was almost full. The row behind us, previously empty, was now occupied by four men in their mid- to late twenties. Having missed the beginning of the game, they apparently did not hear the announcement from the Dodgers that this was a family event and that they should avoid using profane language. These guys were fairly loud, and their talk was punctuated with what some would call "colorful metaphors." The children's eyebrows went up several times as the men discussed a variety of subjects from women at work to the players on the field. The one constant of their banter was salty language, and it wasn't particularly pleasant for the kids to be assaulted by it.

Yet the verbal barrage from behind literally took a backseat to a different problem in front of us. The little kid with the electronic game had stopped playing and become quite cranky. He was whining that the game's batteries were dead, and the little professor, Jin Uk, quipped quietly to me that the boy's batteries were probably running low too. After all, it was awfully late for a child of kindergarten age to be out.

To fix the problem, the men with the crying child took the easy way out: they bought him a toy. A vendor peddling souvenirs had been hawking goodies down our aisle, and the little boy was given a large Dodger flag, which consisted of a two-foot-long wooden stick with a large blue-and-white Dodger pennant attached to it. Naturally, the child began waving it wildly. This did not bother his chaperones, who were barely watching the game or the child anyway. But the flag was persistently being thrust about in such a way that our view was compromised. For the time being, we all decided to say nothing, hoping that the child would grow tired of flailing away. Settling on this course of action was a group process. The children and I glanced at one another, and had a conversation with eyes only. Austin, our wise class clown, wanted me to do something. As he was sitting in the middle of our group, he was the one most affected by the annoying banner in front of him and the stream of F-bombs coming at him from behind. Eventually, though, he acquiesced to the will of the majority and remained silent.

This was another teachable moment. I had no idea at the time that things would turn ugly later, but I knew this little decision would eventually be a topic of conversation with the kids. The incident would be an opportunity to teach children that we all make more choices each day than we realize. Some schools do a fine job teaching kids that actions have consequences and that making the correct call takes practice. Yet for many kids, the process of decision making is not addressed often enough. If selecting the right course of action was easy, youngsters would not constantly find themselves in bad situations. Teaching how to choose the best road is tough, which is exactly why it needs to be highlighted and constantly evaluated and reinforced.

Children need to be aware that they see decisions being made every day—in literature, in movies, and, most important, in real life. These choices—and the consequences they produce—can be chewed, swallowed, and digested, such that each time students make a decision of their own, they can use the knowledge from the sum total of the decisions they have witnessed to help them choose the best path.

Austin is small and was having trouble seeing the game. Bearing his frustration with a patient shrug, he did the best he could, trusting that his feelings would be addressed later. He most likely asked himself what Linda would do if faced with a similar dilemma. Linda was a high school senior who had taken a special interest in Austin when she returned occasionally to visit Room 56.

She was also the poster child for sensational. The kids admired her for beating odds that often defeat others. There was no father in her life, and no money. She lived with her mother and older sister in one of the two bedrooms of a dilapidated apartment; another family used the larger of the two rooms. Linda's mother was a caring and hardworking woman, but easily rattled and unable to find decent employment because she was an illegal alien. Linda's older sister was a loving and bright young woman, but she had been sidetracked by a bad relationship.

These factors stacked the deck against Linda, and made her impressive success inspiring. She was intelligent but not a genius. In elementary school, she chose to take advantage of every extra class offered, including orchestra, additional math study, and Shakespeare. It paid off. With her friend Tracy, she was offered a huge scholarship to an outstanding private school. She counseled Austin and the other children in the class that the secret to success was the ability to make the right choice, time and time again.

## Linda and Ike

We encourage our kids to do the right thing, but they are not always equipped with the tools to do so. Decision making is a skill to be learned and developed in the same way one learns to play a piano. It takes time and practice. Linda had learned in Room 56 a system by which she evaluated her options. In her notebook, she carried a quote from President Dwight Eisenhower: "Plans are nothing; planning is everything."

Linda agreed, and to make plans she took sheets of paper and divided them into two columns by making vertical lines down the center of each page. Each time an important decision presented itself, the consequences of various choices were divided on the sheet into pros and cons. Linda pointed out to younger students like Austin that hundreds of decisions are made every day, about everything from which vegetable to eat with lunch to how much time will be spent studying for a math test. Successful kids, she advised, identify and evaluate options. They weigh a set of facts carefully before choosing a direction. For each option, Linda always considered these questions before entering pros and cons on her paper:

- Will this choice help me achieve my personal goals?
- Will this choice hurt people I love?
- Am I making this choice for myself (level 6 thinking) or am I trying to please someone else (level 3)?
- What will I have to sacrifice if I make this choice?
- Will this decision affect people I do not know (either for good or for bad)?
- Are there financial factors to consider?

Of course, Linda made her share of mistakes growing up. Everyone does. But she didn't make them often, and the choices she made regarding the big issues were consistently good ones. Young people need to identify the process of evaluating options as an essential skill if they are to be competent when the deciding begins. Linda did just that, and it has made all the difference.

## Middle of the Fourth

In *The Merchant of Venice*, Portia is a frustrated young woman, trapped by a rule in her father's will forbidding her to choose a husband. She instead will be won as a prize in a lottery. She mourns her fate, but realizes that in passing harsh judgment on her father's wisdom she needs to consider her own shortcomings: "I can easier teach twenty what were good to be done than to be one of the twenty to follow mine own teaching."

It's easy to wax on to children about the importance of good decision making. It is likewise humbling to make poor decisions right in front of them.

The Cardinals didn't score, but the little boy with the flag had discovered a new use for his toy. After mastering the skill of waving the pennant from side to side, he realized it could also be brandished forward and backward. On several backswings, the flag stick poked me and came close to hitting one of the students. With a break in the action, I considered asking one of the boy's handlers to perhaps talk to him about his flag. I began making a mental list of pros and cons, factoring in the amount of beer being consumed by the men. One possibility was to say nothing and hope the boy would grow tired and stop, but the end did not appear to be in sight. President Teddy Roosevelt said: "In any moment of decision the best thing you can do is the right thing, the next best is the wrong thing, and the worst thing you can do is nothing."

Respecting the Rough Rider's wisdom, I decided to take his advice and hoped my choice would be the right one. No such luck:

RAFE:            (leaning forward and dodging the waving stick) Sir? Excuse me, sir?

MAN:             (annoyed) What?

RAFE:            Sorry to bother you. Would it be possible for you to take his flag away? He keeps accidentally hitting us, and . . .

SECOND MAN:      (screaming) Jesus Christ! He's a goddamn kid! A goddamn kid! What the hell do you know about it, you piece of shit! Just shut the fuck up!

The fans in our section were simultaneously watching and pretending not to notice. The scene had the fascination of a train wreck, and some onlookers no doubt wondered if the man's belligerence would translate to physical violence.

RAFE:            (backing down, with the kids present) Okay, okay! Sorry to disturb you. Just thought I might ask. No worries.

THIRD MAN:       Stop belaboring the point. You belabor everything. You belabor everything. I mean everything. Just shut up!

An amusing thing happened as the men were yelling at me. They were so busy getting in my face that they did not notice as the boy continued to wave his flag and accidentally poked a woman who was walking down the aisle. She turned to say something, but upon seeing the men, she shot me a glance and kept walking.

The incident shook the kids up a bit. To make matters worse, as the bottom of the fourth began, the men intentionally stood up and talked with one another, doing everything in their power to block our view. Nice guys.

Even bad moments have their silver lining. I had tried, as Paul McCartney once advised, to "take a sad song and make it better" and failed miserably. It only underscored the importance and difficulty of making the correct call on a close play.

## Bottom of the Fourth

*Turning to the Dark Side*

Sadly, teaching children the skill of making decisions often involves facing unpleasant realities. In school, well-meaning teachers encourage kids by saying, "We're all winners here." It's a beautiful thought, but it's not always true. People lose all the time. Actions have consequences, and those outcomes are not always pretty. It is necessary for young people—in their studies, but even more so in real life—to examine decisions made by others that have led to awful results.

The purpose of this is not to judge anyone. People who make good decisions are not necessarily better human beings than those who have fallen down and brought harm upon themselves or others. Children should not be encouraged to throw stones. But they need to see, as painful as it may be to do so, that some choices affect us forever and have consequences that cannot be undone.

Austin and his friends had heard about a classmate of Linda's named Karen. She was very beautiful, with a way about her that several teachers at school described as "elegant." Karen was talented, shining in the school orchestra and plays. Her academic performance demonstrated a skill set far above her grade level. There was no reason for this star not to fulfill every parent's dream: that her child should have a better life than she does. Karen's home situation was better than Linda's. Her family did not have to share an apartment and Karen's mother was a legal citizen. As in Linda's house, the father was absent. However, her mother's legal status made it possible for her to work better jobs with more convenient hours and more money. Karen had plenty of attention and guidance.

Despite all she had going for her, Karen made poor choices when middle school began. Like so many good kids, she succumbed to the pressures of adolescence. By age twelve, she had taken to using a lot of makeup and many older guys were paying close attention. Karen went to the local public school, rejecting the very real possibility that with sacrifice she could have attended a more challenging magnet or private school. While Linda was at home filling out application forms, Karen was hanging out with a steady stream of boys at the local park. One didn't have to be a fortune teller to be able to predict her future.

Karen had a baby when she was fifteen. Currently, school is not part of her life. If she was a bad person, it would be easy to dismiss her situation and moralize that "she had it coming." That, however, is not the truth. Karen was and remains a very good girl who made a terrible decision, one that radically altered the landscape of her life and closed many doors in her future.

While young students should be discouraged from judging people or calling them out personally, they need to hear about real individuals whose decisions changed their lives for better or worse. Only by having this information can they get a sense of the profound consequences that life's decisions can have.

Let's be clear. Karen's life is not over. There are outstanding programs to help young mothers, get them back into school, and improve their future. That said, youngsters need to face reality, and the truth is that the day Karen became pregnant the chances of her reaching extraordinary heights were drastically reduced. According to the March of Dimes, only 40 percent of unmarried women under eighteen who have babies graduate from high school, as opposed to 75 percent from the same socioeconomic background who do not. In addition, 78 percent of the babies born to teenagers live in poverty, as opposed to only 9 percent who are born to married women with a high school diploma. These statistics predict a harsh reality for Karen and her son. His opportunity to make good choices has been limited by his mother's disastrous one.

# A Backpack for Roads Less Traveled

Parents walk a fine line between being too involved with their child or not involved enough. Children need to become self-sufficient and lead their own lives. Before they declare independence, though, it can't hurt to fill their satchel with information that can be useful to them when making a choice.

## Tinsel Town Decisions

Hollywood masterpieces can play a part in shaping a child's thought processes when it comes to decision making. As we learn from a character's wise or foolish decisions, we gain knowledge to use in our own lives. And knowledge is power. There are endless good films in which crucial decisions are made that offer constructive lessons about choice and consequence. In the spirit of the Academy Awards, here are three films submitted for your consideration.

Once when James Stewart was discussing *It's a Wonderful Life,* the 1946 Frank Capra landmark that has become one of our culture's most beloved films, he pointed out his favorite scene in the movie. What's interesting about his choice is that this particular scene is not one of the film's classic moments. Normally, highlight montages of the film include the scene in which Stewart's character, George Bailey, contemplates suicide on the bridge, the scene with him running through Bedford Falls, or the movie's joyous close, when Bailey sings "Auld Lang Syne" with his family.

Instead of these, Stewart asked viewers to notice an earlier scene at the train station. George has kept his promise, unhappily supervising the family business following the death of his father. His younger brother, Harry, has gone off to college. George will get to pursue his dreams when Harry returns from school, a college graduate ready to assume stewardship of the Bailey Bros. Building and Loan Association.

But at the train station, Harry arrives with a new wife. Her father has a good job ready for Harry, meaning that George will have to continue running the company. As Harry's family rushes offscreen, George is left there alone. He knows all of his plans of the last four years are for naught. It's an awful moment for a man who has thought only of others, and it seems terribly unfair that no one thinks of him.

Though disaster has struck, George does not make any rash decisions, and he remains true to himself. Difficult as it is, he decides to support his family and community at the cost of possibly never achieving his own dreams of world travel and adventure. The film is much darker than many expect a Capra film to be. George becomes so bitter that he considers suicide, but finally decides during his darkest hour that life is indeed worth living. It is not until much later that George realizes that he is, indeed, "the richest man in town." And though the movie does have a happy ending, Stewart's choice of the train station scene is instructional. It's good for young people to see and discuss that dreams do not always come true; life can be cruel and unfair, and marked by disappointment, even for those who constantly try to do the right thing.

For mature high schoolers, Oliver Stone's _Wall Street_ will provoke discussion over the fate of a young man who clearly does the _wrong_ thing. Charlie Sheen's character, Bud Fox, is a young stockbroker seduced by slimy billionaire Gordon Gekko, wonderfully played by Michael Douglas in an Academy Award–winning performance. For teaching purposes, the movie gets at a point that is too often ignored: all of us make our share of poor decisions that in the worst circumstances might even bring shame and dishonor to ourselves and those around us. Many films focus on a protagonist who makes a wise decision and lives happily ever after. Such is not the case here, as Bud Fox makes a series of terrible decisions that land him in prison. This is a good film to teach decision making because of the character Lou Mannheim, an older broker played by the always marvelous Hal Holbrook. It's good for young people to accept the fact that we all make poor choices, but how we handle those moments of despair can mean the difference between a better future and no future at all. You don't have to care about Wall Street or the stock market to underscore the advice Mannheim gives to Bud as the young man is about to be arrested for insider trading: "Bud, I like you. Just remember, a man looks into the abyss, there's nothing staring back at him. At that moment a man finds his character. And that is what keeps him out of the abyss."

It's okay to tell your children that they will have their moments staring into the abyss despite their best efforts to make good choices. *Wall Street* is a good reminder that poor choices can be followed by brave ones, and that there can be light even at the end of a very dark tunnel.

In the final analysis, exceptional kids make good choices when facing the toughest of decisions. And many of these decisions are made under less-than-ideal circumstances. Peer pressure is hard enough to deal with. When the demands of societal norms are thrown onto the scales, it is no wonder very few kids have the strength to be true to themselves and their beliefs. It is so hard to be different, which often requires standing up to the ridicule and judgment of others.

Teaching kids to go their own way and instilling in them the courage to do so is vital. Stanley Kramer's film adaptation of *Inherit the Wind* has a monologue that is used in Room 56 to drive home this point, not only in the specific context of the Scopes Monkey Trial but as an example for the life of every student.

Spencer Tracy plays Henry Drummond, a lawyer based on Clarence Darrow, who comes to Tennessee to defend Bert Cates for teaching evolution in school. The small town is out for blood, and Cates's girlfriend, Rachel, begs him to apologize in hopes that the town will forget the whole affair. She is angry with Drummond over his insistence on pressing forward with the trial, believing he does not understand that after everything is over she and Bert will have to remain in the small town, hated by all. Drummond has an answer for her fears, one that young people need to consider:

> I know what Bert is going through. It's the loneliest feeling in the world—it's like walking down an empty street listening to the sound of your own footsteps. But all you have to do is to knock on any door and say, "If you let me in I'll live the way you want me to live and I'll think the way you want me to think." And all the blinds will go up and all the doors will open and you'll never be lonely, ever again. Now, it's up to you.

Kids need to know that the tough choice Bert faces is one that all young people will face eventually. Many will decide to go with the flow and compromise their own beliefs to fit in. *Inherit the Wind* will challenge them to do better. It echoes Polonius from *Hamlet*: "This above all, to thine own self be true."

## Literature, Chasing Rabbits, and Going to Hell

Reading outstanding literature is a surefire way to keep the issue of decision making on the front burner. Most protagonists in classic novels are faced with choices that remain relevant to young readers today.

Choosing anything involves sacrifice. An important concept for children to keep in mind is what economists call *opportunity cost*. Many young people want to have everything, but it's necessary to understand that if you want to go to medical school you will have to give up going to some parties that other kids enjoy.

In our society, where entitlement seems to have replaced pursuit, this lesson must be emphasized.

An anonymous philosopher once wrote: "If you chase two rabbits, both will escape."

All readers, young and old, should consider taking the time to read or reread *Oh, the Places You'll Go!* by Dr. Seuss. It is often read during benchmark occasions like school graduations, but its lesson endures throughout life. Seuss's fantastic illustrations dazzle the eye and capture the mood. There are scary moments when the reader is faced with hundreds of roads crisscrossing the page. As Seuss warns us:

You'll look up and down streets. Look 'em over with care.
About some you will say, "I don't choose to go there."

Seuss reinforces the lesson that choices are necessary to move forward, but that taking one path always means forgoing others. It's a book to be read again and again, and students can measure their intellectual and emotional growth from the previous time they read it. Often, they'll find that while the book has not changed, they have.

Most middle school students are force-fed Shakespeare's *Romeo and Juliet.* Fortunate young scholars may have a good teacher who is excited to guide them through this play, but many are taught by someone who covers the book merely because it is on his school district's mandatory reading list.

Hopefully that won't be the case. But in any event, read Shakespeare's first indisputable masterpiece with your child, and follow it up with the remarkable 1968 film adaptation directed by Franco Zeffirelli.

Typical assessments given students in school ask mundane or irrelevant questions about the play. Kids are asked to name Romeo's cousin or Juliet's age. But if a child is to take away something truly meaningful, the questions they are asked must be more probing, and must get at the larger issues the play brings up.

The most important theme on which to focus is the cause of the senseless tragedy at the play's climax. The deaths of the young lovers are caused not by their feuding families or an act of God but by the couple's inability to look before they leap. Romeo and Juliet are young, and unlike the lucky children who have *you* for their parent, they were not schooled in the art of making decisions. Had they listened to Friar Lawrence ("wisely and slow; they stumble that run fast") the two might have lived happily ever after instead of bringing about their own untimely deaths inside Capulet's tomb.

For older students, *The Adventures of Huckleberry Finn* can be the most inspirational story of all. Too often it is assigned to students who read it on their own at a time when they are not yet capable of understanding Twain's genius without help. Just as Huck needs Jim to guide him, even good students need an escort to fully appreciate the pain and brilliance of Huck's final decision.

Huck is a young boy, unwashed and uneducated. Running away from an abusive father, he joins forces with Jim, a slave who is fleeing a cruel and hypocritical society. After the two have numerous adventures on the Mississippi River, Jim is resold into slavery by two frauds known as the King and the Duke. In chapter 31, Huck has to make a decision that will follow him forever: he can follow society's rules and turn Jim over to his owner, or steal Jim out of slavery and free him.

Huck decides to play by the rules and even prays to God to help him do the "right" thing. He writes a letter to Jim's former owner,

Miss Watson, to make himself feel better. But, like Claudius in *Hamlet*, Huck learns "you can't pray a lie." Huck makes his list of pros and cons, and realizes that all of his reasons to betray Jim are rooted in society's beliefs, and not his own. Finally, he looks at the letter he has written and makes a glorious pronouncement:

> It was a close place. I took it up, and held it in my hand. I was a trembling, because I'd got to decide, forever, betwixt two things, and I knowed it. I studied a minute, sort of holding my breath, and then says to myself: 'All right, then, I'll go to hell'—and tore it up.

In that sentence Huck not only makes a decision but demonstrates that he has fully considered the consequences of both courses of action. He has understood that going to hell will be harder than turning in Jim to Miss Watson, but in bravely making the more difficult choice, Huck is accepting personal responsibility for his actions.

Special young people grow up to be like Huck: decisive, moral, and courageous enough to do the right thing even if it means standing alone. In Huck Finn, kids learn perhaps the most important thing about choices: the biggest ones are often the hardest and the loneliest, but those with courage and conviction find the strength to take the hard road where others choose the easier path.

Finally, *To Kill a Mockingbird*, Harper Lee's Pulitzer Prize–winning novel, serves as a sort of family bible in Room 56. There is not a page without humor, truth, and wisdom. When children practice making decisions, remind them that in the final analysis choices have to be their own, reached by weighing their options against the backdrop of all the knowledge they have gathered in life so far. For their difficult decisions, when the weight of the world seems too much to bear, please arm with them Atticus Finch's advice regarding the pressure to conform: "But before I live with other people I have to live with myself. The one thing that doesn't abide by majority rule is a person's conscience."

## End of the Fourth

The game was almost half over. The Dodgers had pushed across another run, making the score 3–2 in favor of the Cardinals. The giant screen entertained the crowd by showing various baseball players either falling or making errors. I looked at the five little ones, laughing with one another and making silly bets about the Dodgers' chances of winning the game. I was pleased that once again they were talking to one another rather than watching a screen—a tiny victory in the world of making wise choices. Millions of decisions awaited them, and I hoped they were prepared to make good ones.

As they sat laughing, my thoughts drifted back to Karen, whom the kids saw pushing a stroller through the neighborhood most nights. She was just a baby, really, pushing a baby. I was still confident that both Karen and her little one would beat the odds and lead productive lives. Karen always had the ability to accomplish something special in her life. Her poor decision had placed serious obstacles in her way, but with age, wisdom, and the support of others, those obstacles could still be overcome.

I also thought about Linda, who would be dreaming tonight about the endless possibilities in front of her. She had worked hard to make the right decisions, and college, career, boyfriends, travel, and a multitude of friends awaited her. Oh, the places she'll go.

# Sweeping Like Shakespeare

## Top of the Fifth

The fifth inning was about to begin and Jessica and Yo Yo wanted to get a bottle of water. It was past nine P.M., and the darkness coupled with the beer consumption of fans around us prompted me to accompany them to the concession stand. The stadium was quite calm, so we anticipated a ten-second stop with a quick exchange of money and an immediate return to our seats. Not a chance.

We hustled up the stairs and found a stand where bottled water was sold. The teenage employee was on her cell phone talking with a friend. It wasn't Thanksgiving, but we couldn't help but think of the scene in *Planes, Trains and Automobiles* in which Steve Martin's frustrated character is trying to rent a car and the lady behind the counter provokes his outrage by making him wait while she giggles on the phone with a family member. At the scene's climax, Martin explodes with a breathtakingly funny torrent of curses. As life imitates art, the attendant selling snacks must have been related to the woman in the film. She was in no hurry to help us. When she finally decided to hang up the phone and do her job, the girls ordered two bottles of water.

"What?" she asked, her voice filled with boredom.

"May we have two bottles of water, please?" repeated the young ladies.

"Yeah . . . hang on a sec."

The employee disappeared behind a side door for at least a minute. She finally returned with a Coke and a box of Cracker Jack.

"I'm sorry," I said, taking over. "The girls wanted some water."

"Oh, yeah, right," replied our server. She returned with the bottles of water, and rang up seven dollars on the cash register. The girls handed her a ten-dollar bill. She took it and gave us five dollars in return.

The kids looked at each other and then at me.

"Um, you gave us too much," said Jessica. "You only owe us three dollars."

"Whatever," the girl replied.

Finally, water in hand and change in our pockets, we returned to our seats. The Cardinals had been busy, putting men on first and third with only one out. The boys had entered the data on our score sheets and brought us up to speed in a matter of seconds.

The contrast between the boys' efficiency with their scorecards and the girls' experience with the bored concession worker prompted another important lesson. Ben Franklin wrote that "anything worth doing is worth doing well." It's never wise to argue with Dr. Franklin, and this sentiment needs to be instilled in our children.

There are many great sayings about the value of work, but one of my favorites comes from Dr. Martin Luther King Jr., who often quoted an anonymous poem about doing one's best. During his inspiring speeches he would paraphrase several sections of the poem, but for our purposes here, let children always remember:

> If it falls your lot to sweep streets,
> Sweep them like Michelangelo painted pictures,
> Like Shakespeare wrote poetry,
> Like Beethoven composed music.

Many people do not take pride in their work. When things go wrong or end up unaccomplished, there's often a lot of finger pointing in the search for a scapegoat. Nobody likes the blame game, but many parts of our society conspire to produce the mediocre work ethic that makes even ordering a couple of bottles of water difficult.

Children need to take pride in all they do. If they're going to sweep the streets, they need to do it like Shakespeare, so to speak. Parents should be aware that school grading policies often play a role in the development of a bad work ethic. In many schools, academic standards have been lowered to make teachers and administrators feel like they are doing a good job. For example, at a recent staff meeting officials reviewed the results from our standardized tests administered the previous year. Their talk was reminiscent of Winston Smith's reports for the Ministry of Truth in George Orwell's novel *1984.*

We were told that our children were doing a fabulous job with numbers. Fabulous? Almost 40 percent of the students did not pass the math test at the end of the year. Because other schools were doing even worse, our campus applauded itself for its "high" scores. No one had the courage or energy to point out that in the real world, failing 40 percent of the time is not considered fabulous. A 40 percent failure rate in the real world means a pink slip, or worse. But when schools proclaim otherwise to project an image of success, it reinforces the wrong message for children.

In fact, these days children are indirectly taught that actions *do not* have consequences. Lawyers have frightened schools to the point where incorrigible children are coddled and passed even when they have not remotely mastered the state requirements.

At Hobart Elementary School, a typical urban public institution, fifth graders graduate each June and move on to middle school. Last year, several gang members in the class openly cursed teachers and peers all through graduation rehearsals. When teachers asked administrators to have these hooligans pulled from the ceremony, they were told that all kids must graduate onstage no matter how poor their behavior or how dismal their academic record.

Leave no child behind? That's ridiculous. Some children *should* be left behind until they're truly ready to move on to the next level. These kids need serious help, and passing them when they are illiterate or failing is not the right thing to do. It sends a terrible message to everyone at the school.

One teacher was told that her gang-attired student was a "good kid." This child constantly hurt other people, disrupted the class, and did absolutely no work. I am sorry, but this is not a good kid. There is the possibility that he will become one someday, but let's be straight. Students who hurt others and fail every subject in school are not anywhere in the neighborhood of being good kids.

Our school has a contest known as Math Field Day. It's a fun event where the classes take a test comprised of all the math skills they are supposed to have mastered. At the end of the competition, all children, some of whom had missed more than half the problems on the exam, are awarded prizes and a pizza party and are told, "We are all winners here."

Nope. Sorry. Not true.

When students take an easy math test and miss 90 percent of the problems, they are not winners. I understand and applaud people's efforts to build up kids' self-esteem, but lying to children does not help them in the long run.

## The Road to Greatness

While all learning begins at home, youngsters can glean so much by observing the people they encounter every day. Watching the work ethic of peers, mentors, and even strangers, whether good or bad, can open the door to important life lessons.

These days it has become politically correct to avoid judging others. The humanity behind this sentiment is well taken, but the truth is that people make many judgments every day. We choose schools, doctors, and barbers based on whether their work meets our standards of excellence. It's a good thing at the end of the day for children to consider all the people they have encountered. Some sweep like Shakespeare and others do not. When kids see the value in a job well done, they can take ownership of this philosophy.

A few months earlier, the students at the game with me were supposed to travel to Arizona to demonstrate their language skills to a large group of dedicated teachers. We all looked forward to the event. It was the sort of performance that meant absolute joy for the children: a trip out of state, performing for friendly teachers, and the chance to see new sights. None of us could have foreseen the nightmare that was about to begin:

8:30 A.M.:   Our plane was to leave LAX at 11:00 A.M. As a group with a lot of travel experience, we arrived at the terminal at 8:30, two and a half hours before the short flight to Phoenix.

8:40 A.M.:   Although we had the tickets in hand, an attendant informed us that there might not be room on the plane. The airline company had oversold the flight. Even though we were the *first* people there for the flight and more than two hours early, an employee had us wait near the ticket terminal, where further instructions would be delivered shortly.

9:30 A.M.:   "Shortly" turned out to be a relative term, as a representative came over to us almost an hour later. They had decided to put us on the plane and we were sent through security.

10:00 A.M.:  We arrived at our gate and sat down in the waiting area. A young woman at the counter called us up. She had received a message from downstairs and was sorry to tell me that they were mistaken. We would not be able to board the flight, but were to return downstairs, where a man named Gary would help us. Although shocked, I had enough of my senses left to ask how our bags, already tagged for the flight, would be returned. Supposedly Gary had all the answers, and was waiting downstairs to take care of us immediately. I tried to get an explanation as to why this was happening, but she laughed and said it was just a crazy day. None of the children thought it was particularly funny.

10:20 A.M.: We arrived downstairs. Gary was there and asked us to wait a moment. He was on the phone fixing things.

11:05 A.M.: Gary smiled and came over. All was resolved. We were told to take a bus from LAX to Burbank (an hour ride) to get on a different plane. He laughed as he said this and told us not to worry. Gary gave us paper vouchers to pay for the bus ride, and additional coupons for the children to get a meal at the Burbank airport before boarding our flight, scheduled to leave at 4:00 P.M.

11:30 A.M.: At the bus waiting area, a man asked what we were doing there. I told him his company representative had instructed us to take the bus to Burbank. He asked me for $140. I gave him the vouchers and he started cracking up. He said they *never* accept vouchers. If John Huston and Humphrey Bogart were there, I would have thought to myself, "Vouchers? We don't need no stinking vouchers!" But it was no laughing matter. I gave the man the money. Anything to get out of there.

12:40 P.M.:  We arrived at Burbank Airport. You guessed it. The meal vouchers were no good.

5:15 P.M.:  The plane touched down in Phoenix. Several of the bags were lost. They were not recovered for more than a week. Many important items needed for the performance were gone.

This was obviously a terrible day, but even catastrophic experiences can be used to instill excellence in children. We spent the evening at the hotel going over the day's events. The kids thought hard about not only the incompetence of many of the employees we encountered, but also their seemingly uncaring attitudes.

At the Arizona school the following morning, the students were welcomed by a well-organized, dedicated group of teachers who went out of their way to roll out the red carpet. Don't think the kids didn't appreciate it. Some people take pride in their jobs and others do not. Traveling is a wonderful way for kids to learn the difference.

## Middle of the Fifth

The Cardinals scored two runs in the top of the inning, increasing their lead to 5–2. Some people headed to the exits with the game barely half over.

Jessica and Ye Rim were erasing their score sheets. They hadn't made any mistakes, but found a way to pencil in the relief pitcher to make their record keeping neater. That they worked with such meticulous care is exactly the point. No one would ever see these sheets. The girls were correcting their own work without even being told to do so. There was no grade involved, and truth be told, within two days these records would probably be in a recycling bin or at the bottom of a drawer. But for special children, excellence is a way of life, not just something to strive for in school, and these two little girls had embraced that philosophy.

## Bottom of the Fifth

Let me reiterate one very important point. The children scoring the game are extraordinary young people, but not because of superior intellect or innate talent. In many ways they are no different from millions of other children across America, and in fact, some of the kids have overcome tremendous odds, avoiding the pitfalls of poverty and broken homes to achieve their success. But they were not born extraordinary. Instead, these children have *become* special because they have parents and teachers guiding them with a consistent message. Most young people never "sweep the streets like Shakespeare" because of mixed messages they receive in their daily lives.

## Rights Versus Privileges

Adults today often complain that young people do not understand that actions have consequences. In school and at home, children often display a frightening attitude of entitlement. But when you consider things from a child's point of view, it makes sense that he might not understand that in this life he is entitled to nothing.

After all, the child did not have to apply to his school: a neighborhood address was the only prerequisite for enrollment. At some schools free breakfast and lunch are offered. Kids are almost never excluded from extracurricular activities. When most schools take field trips, all children go—students who misbehave in class or fail to turn in work still get on the bus. Teachers are often frustrated because the power to discipline kids when necessary has been taken away by bureaucratic forces operating from a "no child left behind" mentality. With their teachers' powers of oversight diminished, many children learn that they can get what they want without really trying. Kids cease to care about the quality of their work because the free meal or trip to the zoo will happen no matter what they have done. This has to stop, and parents and teachers can work together to make it happen.

A few years ago an interesting incident occurred with the students I teach on Saturday mornings. There were about fifty scholars in the class, ranging from grades six through nine. The kids study Shakespeare, reading comprehension, algebra, and vocabulary. Those who do well in their regular school as well as on Saturday mornings are invited to come to the Oregon Shakespeare Festival the following summer.

Mary was one of the sixth graders. As happens with the onset of adolescence, she lost some of her focus when she began middle school. Her study habits were not as strong as they should have been, and she missed some Saturday sessions. At the end of the year, I met with Mary and her mother, and explained that the young lady had not earned the right to go to the Shakespeare festival.

Mama and daughter cried. The mother was upset but polite, and promised me she would counsel her daughter when they went home.

One of Mary's classmates was Christine, who quit the Saturday program in the middle of the year. When this happened, I called Christine's mother to explain that quitting the class was a mistake. Children should learn that when they make a commitment they need to follow through. Quitting is a dangerous habit. Christine's mother disagreed, and that was that.

After we returned from the Shakespeare festival early the next summer, I heard from both girls. Mary came in to talk to me. She admitted her classroom performance had been poor, and asked to continue studying on Saturdays when fall classes resumed. I gave her a schedule and told her I would be thrilled to see her back at work.

Surprisingly, I heard from Christine as well, almost six months after she quit the program. Her main reason for contacting me was to ask if her younger sister, a fourth grader, could take guitar lessons from me over the summer. I found a guitar for her sister, who then participated in free music lessons with about thirty other kids. After six weeks of instruction, the girl quit the class. She didn't like practicing because it was hard.

With fall approaching, students began to sign up for the Saturday classes. Although the schedule had been available to all the kids for the entire summer, I received an e-mail from Christine at midnight on the Friday before the classes were to begin. She was planning to return. I wrote back that night expressing my concern that it might not be right for her because it was a serious class for serious students. She was still welcome to come, but I expected her to finish what she started. I finished the reply around 12:15 A.M.

and went to bed to try to catch a few hours of sleep before begin-ning the new class later that morning.

Up at 4:45 A.M., I checked my e-mail and found a message from Christine. If I wasn't fully awake before I turned on my com-puter, I certainly was after reading her message. It was short and to the point, full of foul language and name calling and on fire with a righteous anger that seemed all the more terrifying coming from a sixth grader. To put it tactfully, Christine informed me in no uncertain terms that she would not be attending the class. And she told me to go to hell.

Raising children can certainly be painful. This was a child whom I had taught for a year, taken to Washington, D.C., and for whom I had paid the tuition to a special summer school. But the anger surfacing came from a misguided sense of entitlement. She had a parent who allowed her to move through life thinking everything is free. It isn't. Things cost. Here are a few suggestions to help drive the message home.

## Carrying Michelangelo and Shakespeare in a Backpack

### Discrimination Is Good

The word *discrimination* has been given a bad rap. Tied up with the shameful history of racism, it has become synonymous with bigotry. But this word also has a positive meaning, describing the ability to make distinctions among various pieces of information. Young people who pursue excellence must learn to discriminate.

Family film nights and literature sessions should focus on qual-ity over quantity. Kids cannot strive for excellence unless they know what it looks like (and what it doesn't look like). Extraordinary kids do not go to the mall to watch a film simply because others at school are talking about it. They have discriminating tastes, and learn to separate substance from hype.

When your child is making choices, have him explain his reasoning to you. As often as possible, support the decision, but encourage the process of discrimination. Whether the decision involves choosing food on a menu, a book in the library, or a toy in a store, children need to consider the benefits of different options. Not all food on the menu is equally tasty. Not all barbers in the shop cut hair with the same skill. Children with discriminating tastes are more likely to reach a little higher.

*Peerless Vision*

I cannot stress it enough: the arts must be a part of every child's life. The responsibility, discipline, and happiness achieved through playing a violin or painting pictures stays with the creator for a lifetime. But in order for children to reach further when it comes to developing musical or artistic talent, they need to be exposed to peers who are working to create similar magic.

I once saw a high school orchestra from a large urban school struggling to make music. Given the children's impoverished backgrounds and lack of experience, they were off to a good start. That's all it was, though—a good start. These young musicians should have been praised, but also given the encouragement to take their playing to the next level. However, their well-intentioned teachers had deluded them into thinking they were the finest high school orchestra in the nation. These students actually believed they would be a part of a philharmonic one day based solely on the level of musicianship they had already reached. The chance of that happening was about the same as my beating Tiger Woods in a game of golf.

These young musicians needed to see other kids their age playing beautifully. For children to be inspired to work hard and achieve greatness, they need to understand that their own world is a small one. Other kids are doing the same thing and achieving more. This is not meant to discourage a child, but to show him reality. It is rare that anyone has greatness thrust upon him. Good young chess players need to play against even better chess players. A child may be one of the best readers in his school, but he needs to understand that there are thousands of schools where kids read at an even more advanced level. Nothing motivates the pursuit of excellence like the truth.

*Going the Extra Mile on Film*

Many good movies have been made about people who take pride in their work. Children of all ages will love Disney's underrated 2002 film *The Rookie*. It is formulaic but still well crafted. There is one short scene in the film that presents a fantastic lesson to be discussed even with small children. The movie's protagonist is a lonely boy who loves baseball but cannot join a team because his father's military job is constantly taking his family around the country. As a result, the young pitcher never gets to pursue his first love.

Alone in a small Texas town, the boy wanders into a store looking for a pair of baseball socks but cannot find what he wants. The store is as lonely and empty as the kid's soul, and he is totally discouraged. But the store owner is sensitive to the youngster's sadness and takes him aside to look at some catalogs to find the precious socks.

Children should take note of the subtle but important lesson in this scene. The owner isn't getting rich here. Many others would ignore the boy and get back to their TV show or snack. But this proprietor does the best he can to help. He knows that every customer counts, and that doing what he can to make the boy happy reflects not only a good deed but a sense of purpose in the life he has chosen for himself. Let your child know that when he works on an assignment or cleans his room, he should tackle the project with the same attitude as this caring adult who helps the sad little boy in ways he cannot possibly know.

Sweeping like Shakespeare isn't easy, especially in a world where tempting shortcuts and overnight success stories can give youngsters false expectations. John Avildsen's 1984 film, *The Karate Kid*, is a nice story to combat these falsehoods. Ralph Macchio's character, Daniel, is a teenager being bullied and wants to learn to defend himself. He is eager to learn karate, but his mentor, Mr. Miyagi, puts him through a series of seemingly useless jobs that increasingly frustrate him. Then, just when he has become fed up with this busy work, Mr. Miyagi shows him that all along he has actually been learning useful skills that will serve as the fundamentals of his karate instruction. In the process of learning to work hard and focus, Daniel learns lessons that go far beyond karate. He has to earn the things he wants, and, to quote Ringo Starr and George Harrison, "It don't come easy."

For older students, or mature younger ones, Steven Spielberg's masterpiece *Saving Private Ryan* is essential viewing. In Room 56 we watch it on Veterans Day. Of course it is a history lesson, and the first twenty minutes present a shockingly realistic look at war of a kind rarely seen on film. But for the purposes of the lessons we are trying to instill in unique children, make sure they understand Colonel Miller's (Tom Hanks) dying line. I have watched the film countless times with young people and they often do not clearly hear his words through all the explosions and noise of the battle. As he dies, Miller tells Private Ryan (Matt Damon), whose life he has saved, to "earn this." We then see Private Ryan fifty years later standing at Miller's grave and looking back on the life he has led. He asks his wife to tell him he is a good man and has led a good life. I want the kids to know that one day they will be older and be faced with the same reflections. Will they have taken pride in what they have done? Will they have done their best? Private Ryan has been given a gift: other men have made the ultimate sacrifice so he might live. In a similar sense, children should understand that others in their lives—parents, teachers, mentors—make sacrifices on a smaller scale so that they, the children, might succeed. The hard work they undertake during their lives shows respect not only for their own time and effort but for those who have sacrificed to give them the opportunities that allowed them to reach for great heights.

It goes hand in hand with Dr. King's request to sweep like Shakespeare. Nothing will be handed to us. We should strive to be the best we can be and to earn everything we wish to possess or achieve.

## The Allowance of Level 6 Thinking

Wise parents want their kids to know the value of money and many give a weekly allowance. This is a good thing. Everyone has a different way of doing it, but most feel that the amount of money should increase with a child's age. Sensible mothers and fathers teach their kids to budget their allowance among spending, saving, and giving. They also allow their young ones to make mistakes. If a child has spent his allowance and does not have enough money left to go to the movies with friends, no rescue should be offered.

The mistake is linking allowance to household chores. It's understandable for parents to think this way because people are paid to work, and it seems like a good lesson to impart to a child. However, household chores should be a gift one gives to the family. Parents are not paid for cooking dinner, and children should not be paid to clean their room or wash a bathroom sink. Kohlberg's second level of moral development points to doing things for a reward, but a level 6 thinker knows that the work is the reward itself. And the better the work is done, the better the reward. A child who keeps his room tidy is more likely to have an organized folder and meticulously completed school assignments. An allowance trains a child in money management, but simultaneously teaches the higher principle that few children understand: a job well done is the highest reward of all.

## The Bill Gates Myth

The amazing Bill Gates is often mistakenly quoted as the creator of the popular set of "Rules for Living." Many believe Gates himself created these rules, but they are actually the work of author and teacher Charles Sykes. It is not Mr. Gates's fault this happened, but let's give credit where it is due. Mr. Sykes has written several books, and although his political views are not for everyone, he has coined some thoughtful and amusing bits of wisdom that children should hear. One of my favorites goes something like this:

> Your school may have done away with winners and losers. Life hasn't. In some schools, they'll give you as many times as you want to get the right answer. Failing grades have been abolished and class valedictorians scrapped, lest anyone's feelings be hurt. . . . This, of course, bears not the slightest resemblance to anything in real life.

Make sure your child understands that his days with you at home and his time at school are helping to prepare him for life. Students like Christine, who wrote me the obscenity-laced note, throw tantrums when they do not get their way. Children must learn that rejection and failure are parts of life, providing a chance to either try again or quit.

## If the Sky's the Limit, Set Some!

If a robber lives in a town with eight banks, and seven are burgle-proof, he will continue to rob the easy target unless someone stops him. Children are the same way. As long as parents and teachers refuse to set limits, kids will follow the path of least resistance. It takes parents and schools reinforcing each other's lessons to really teach children to take pride in all they do.

Teachers are often frustrated when they feel parents aren't doing enough to encourage children to do their best work. Likewise, some outstanding parents are frustrated when they feel the bar in school is set too low. Setting limits and expectations must be a joint effort.

Educators need to return assignments to children when they are not up to snuff. If a student receives a low grade, the only thing he learns is that he did his work badly. He should be made to redo the assignment until it reaches higher standards. Make sure the student knows that mediocrity has no place in class or in life.

Parents need to have kids redo chores if the work is slipshod or incomplete. If dishes are not properly washed or laundry is folded poorly, have them tackle these chores again until the job is done correctly. The earlier this process starts, the better. I am not advocating a sober, joyless, military-style education. Nowhere will you hear more laughter than in Room 56. But it is an educated laughter, coming from children who are happy and confident that they fulfill the highest of expectations in everything they do.

## End of the Fifth

The Cardinals continued to hold their lead. The Dodgers had a brief moment of hope, but a double play ended the inning with the Cardinals up by three. The kids were all a little sad, seeing their home team down by several runs and struggling to come back. Cesar remarked that the game was still close. He realized that there is an incredibly fine line between winning and losing— the outcome was by no means decided. One hit here or one extra strike could make the difference. I reminded him that life is a lot like that.

While the kids filled in their score sheets, I thought about my own statistics: plenty of losses and not enough wins. It would be nice if it were simply a matter of good kids and bad ones, but anyone with sense realizes it's not that simple. Here were five sensational youngsters who were buying into a lifestyle of high expectations and self-imposed demands for excellence. It was hard to feel good about their bright futures when I thought of Christine, who had once filled out scorecards in the same seats occupied by this newer generation. One thing is for sure: we have to keep pitching Dr. King's challenge. Great hopes can lead to heartbreaking defeats, but there are times when the message gets through.

Not all young people melt down when limits are imposed. Mary, whom I had once held back from going to the Oregon Shakespeare Festival because of her mediocre work, was doing brilliantly in high school. She had written me a funny e-mail earlier in the year, teasing me about my nagging her to aim higher:

Dear Rafe:

This is Mary! Sorry I haven't come to visit you and the new class. I was thinking about those days because I met a teacher who knows us and comes to watch our Shakespeare plays. He thinks it's amazing that little kids can perform unabridged Shakespeare. He also remembered many of the songs he heard our class sing. I am so thankful that I was in your class, and I wanted to say thanks to you for being tough on me.

Rafe, you gave me many opportunities. You always told me to "sweep the streets like Shakespeare," but I wanted to tell you something you should add when you nag the little ones. If you follow that advice, you won't have to sweep the streets! You'll have better opportunities than that! I plan to be a veterinarian, and I promise you, I'll be the best one I can be.

Some things work out. Let's credit a wise mother who did not allow her daughter to wallow in self-pity when she lost some privileges. Mary faced a united front from her teacher and parents, who told her that the pursuit of happiness requires sacrifice and effort, and that those who think they are entitled are sadly mistaken. Thanks to her hard work, I don't doubt that some sick and injured animals will one day be in the hands of an excellent veterinarian. And, to quote that old saying, Mary will have achieved her success the old-fashioned way: she'll have earned it.

# All About Eve

The leadoff hitter for the Cardinals in the top of the sixth inning fouled off a pitch and sent the ball screaming into our section, a few rows away from us. The ball hit the aisle stairway, and bounced high into the air. As it came down, it was headed straight toward a little boy, about eight, who was watching the game with his dad. The boy had brought his glove and was just about to catch the ball when a grown man fell on top of him trying to gobble it up. The interloper snatched his treasure and returned to his seat several rows away as the father leaned over and consoled his son.

Selfishness.

It comes in various shapes and sizes, and it's understandable, though often disappointing. Human beings are selfish by nature. Extraordinary children learn to see beyond themselves, but teaching empathy and selflessness is no easy task. For this reason, parents and teachers need to spend as much time as it takes to help kids come to the realization that they are not the center of the universe. Perhaps then one day the little boy will be allowed to catch the ball rather than end up trampled by the lout who almost ruined his evening.

Fortunately, Austin came to the rescue. As guests of the Dodgers, my students had been brought onto the field to watch batting practice before the game, and one of the coaches was kind enough to give each child a baseball. In fact, each student was given a gift bag filled with a variety of baseball goodies. This generosity on the part of the Dodgers inspired Austin to walk down the aisle and give his baseball to the little boy, who was instantly made happy again. The grateful father watched Austin return to his seat, and gave me an appreciative nod.

President Kennedy inspired a country with his inaugural address, and the speech's key phrase was a call for selflessness. He challenged his fellow Americans to put their individual desires aside and to ask what they could do for their country. This dynamic speech is shown anytime JFK is in the news. It's a rousing call to arms, and provides excellent motivation for parents and teachers facing the daunting task of explaining altruism to a youngster whose natural inclinations run in the opposite direction. A good parent or teacher can help a child understand that selflessness brings great rewards, but these benefits are not often immediately apparent. At times, teaching children not to be self-centered may seem counterintuitive to them. It takes time and effort to develop a selfless kid, one with the ability to see a greater good outside his window.

Though Austin was not showy about giving the child his ball, the people around us noticed. Several approving adults in the stands gave Austin smiles and a thumbs-up. These admirers seemed to comment, "Wouldn't it be nice if more people were like this kid?"

Yet Austin would be the first person to downplay his act of charity. There was a time when giving up his ball would not have crossed his mind. Over the last year he had readjusted the scope of his vision to include others and this change had not been a natural one. Children do not simply outgrow selfishness; in fact, egocentric children often mature into self-centered adults. Altruism is an important trait that must be taught, the earlier the better. As with all the lessons in this book, change is obtained gradually in the developing child through a constant series of lessons and reminders. Star Trek fans will quote Leonard Nimoy's character, Mr. Spock, in *The Wrath of Khan*, who once reminded Captain Kirk that "the needs of the many outweigh the needs of the few."

## All for One and One for All

In some classes, particularly those involved with an art-related project like a play or a concert, standard procedure is to split up the students according to the roles they will play in the production. Drama teachers often rehearse only with the students they will "need" that day to go through a certain set of scenes. This happens in the worlds of sports and music as well. Teachers understandably employ this strategy to give more individual attention to the kids with whom they are working. However, this is a missed opportunity to teach something far more important than the content of whatever show or concert is in rehearsal.

When our class spends a year producing a Shakespeare play, the entire cast comes to all rehearsals. It is true that there are times when certain kids sit around for more than an hour watching others rehearse. There may be a dance practice or the blocking of a scene that involves only ten to twelve students while forty others watch. But the reason that everyone attends is to help the kids overcome their selfish tendencies. The key is something we discussed earlier: focus. Those who aren't part of the scene at hand are not allowed to drift or goof around; they need to pay attention. It is imperative that the kids spend time watching others work and fail and sweat before reaching excellence. After a while something wonderful happens—students begin to smile and take great joy in the achievement of others. It may be more "effective" to work only with specific children, but that is based on the assumption that the show is the most important thing. It's not. The kids are. Teaching them to root for their peers and embrace the progress of others is a far more important goal than a standing ovation that lasts for a few minutes. Seeing beyond oneself can last a lifetime.

This point was taught to me in 1987 when Sir Ian McKellen was gracious enough to bring my students to San Diego to watch his brilliant one-man play, entitled *Acting Shakespeare*. After the show, Sir Ian packed the kids into his dressing room backstage and asked them how many people were in the play. The children were puzzled before giving what seemed to be the obvious answer of "one."

"That's not true," Ian gently chided. He then introduced more than twenty people working behind the scenes. "This is Robert, who sold tickets today. Here is Wendy, who got my tea ready for me. And here's Susan, who ran the lights." The actor went on for several minutes, and the kids listened and began nodding their heads in understanding. The room became very quiet, with all eyes fixed on the great actor as he summarized the lesson: "There are no one-man shows."

# Handsome, Brilliant, and Worthless

Selfishness appears in many forms. Its most common expression is found in people who want more than their reasonable share. It's the kid who demands more than his equal share of time or attention, or wants the extra slice of pizza when some haven't even had their first. The problem is often related to poor vision; such kids simply do not realize that there are other people around them.

Joseph was a brilliant and highly motivated kid destined for great things. He was handsome, friendly, and extremely funny. Despite all these attributes, he was ordinary. Selfishness can do that to a person.

It doesn't make Joseph a bad kid, but his self-centered behavior often kept him from being his best. There is so much more to success in life than high test scores and grade point averages. Joseph had the potential for greatness, but even highly successful students have something to learn.

As a young man, Joseph won a scholarship to an elite boarding school. One night, some of the students behaved badly, breaking campus rules. Like many teenagers, the kids didn't think about the ramifications of their actions. When the transgressions were discovered, their parents had to be called by the administrators, and the reputation of the school took a hit. Joseph was one of the offenders. His parents were shocked when they were told that if certain regulations were disregarded again he might even be expelled; despite the trouble, Joseph's grades were still excellent. The fact that he was basically a very good kid was not enough to prevent him from doing something incredibly stupid.

Sometimes, even a serious lesson doesn't quite sink in. Although Joseph was truly sorry for the incident, his "me first" philosophy remained unchanged. More than a year later, he was part of a group of twenty high school students touring colleges with me. At the University of Pennsylvania I offered to buy the kids souvenirs. Standing by the cash register, I soon became a Christmas tree decorated with various T-shirts, pennants, and caps. Joseph selected an outrageously expensive sweatshirt with a price tag at least three times the value of anything the other students had chosen. After piling it into my already sagging arms, he asked if he could get a second item. One look from me gave him the answer. Joseph had much to learn, despite his high-powered brain and impressive résumé. It's not easy getting a kid with the world at his feet to *think* about the world, but it is a necessary task if a child is to fulfill his extraordinary potential. At the time, I was frustrated with Joseph, as I felt he hadn't learned a thing about rejecting selfishness. As you will see later, I would turn out to be completely wrong.

## Middle of the Sixth

The stadium's cameras now focused on fans who were busting out their best dance moves in the shallow hope of receiving five seconds of face time on the big screen. A woman in our section was shown on the screen, and then spent fifteen minutes on her cell phone calling every person she knew to let them share in her glory.

Interestingly, one of the camera crews came to our row, though they couldn't have known that one of the girls, Jessica, was an outstanding dancer. Our class gets to work with a brilliant choreographer named Sarah Scherger, one of those amazing teachers who is able to combine hard work with tons of fun. I asked Jessica if she wanted to dance for the camera, but she quietly declined.

"Sarah taught me not to show off," explained Jessica quietly, "and we're not here to do a show. We're here for the Dodgers."

She's quite a kid. The Dodgers may have been losing, but for my money the evening was going very well indeed.

## Bottom of the Sixth

The Dodgers remained three runs behind. Neither of the starting pitchers was still in the game, and the kids looked forward to the upcoming frame. Some of the Dodgers' weaker hitters were coming up, but little kids live in hope.

The images of the "fifteen minutes of fame" crowd still danced in my head. No wonder it is so difficult to inspire kids to have a generosity of spirit. Our social culture *promotes* egotistical behavior. Athletes and pop stars behave outrageously and grab headlines while the world's serious issues are ignored. We have reached a point where people are famous for being celebrities rather than having accomplished anything meaningful.

There are even more insidious aspects to selfishness that children need to understand and avoid. Most youngsters can be taught that basic greed (sorry, Gordon Gekko) is not good. However, other forms of selfishness need to be identified. For example, there is self-centered behavior that results in pettiness, and a more dangerous strand of egotism that involves the manipulation of others. All forms must be cataloged and filed in a kid's backpack. He needs to recognize the enemy, and too often the enemy comes from within us.


## Insect Authority

George Orwell warned us about it in *Animal Farm*. Ray Davies of the Kinks sang about it in his song "20th Century Man." More recently, comedian Ricky Gervais satirized it in *The Office*. Selfishness is everywhere, and one of the worst forms it can take is insect authority. Everyone, even small children, occasionally runs into someone who allows power to corrupt and cloud their common sense. I have seen third graders wet their pants when they were prevented from using a bathroom because they did not have a hall pass. There's nothing wrong with taking a job as hall monitor seriously, but even young children need to learn that power presents the opportunity to be either benevolent or selfish.

Every child will one day find himself in a job with a set of responsibilities to fulfill or carry out. How he approaches these responsibilities can have meaningful consequences. To be charged with a job is to be given some degree, however large or small, of power, and children need to learn to make thoughtful decisions about how to apply that power. Will they use it selfishly as a weapon against others in order to feel better about themselves? Or will they realize, like Spider-Man, that "with great power comes great responsibility"? It's essential to help children see that not every rule is hard and fast, and that authority commands no respect without good judgment. To think only of oneself when the happiness or success of others is at stake is a kind of selfishness that all kids should be taught to avoid.

Austin and I had recently talked about how he missed one of his favorite teachers, who had quit teaching when some misguided supervisors continued to hassle her for not precisely following the daily schedule prescribed by the administration. The fact that incredible things were happening in the classroom was ignored by these supervisors. They seemed more concerned with selfishly exerting their authority than taking the time to see how the teacher's valuable lessons might be expanded to reach greater numbers of students. The people with the clipboards watched but could not see. The danger is that children, unless taught otherwise, often grow up to imitate the selfish behavior they see in adults. But if we are careful to help kids see how hurtful the results of this selfishness can be, we can inspire them to do better when one day they are the ones holding the clipboard.

The departure of his beloved teacher was just one of the things that had helped Austin understand the negative effects of selfishness. The lesson had probably also contributed to his decision to give his baseball to the little kid at the start of the inning. A victim of the collateral damage selfishness can inflict, Austin had recognized the disease and provided the cure.

## The Oxymoron of Selfish Philanthropy

Every Christmas Eve, the Hobart Shakespeareans go to a church to help feed and distribute clothing to the homeless while entertaining them with Christmas carols. The children have noticed that some of the volunteers at such events are grouchy and seem uncaring. It brings up a troubling point: even people attending charitable functions are not always there for righteous reasons. Over the years, the kids have witnessed some remarkable acts of selfishness at a place where the opposite impulse is the whole point. Adults have actually seized plates of food from younger servers and prevented them from feeding the hungry. They do this, strangely enough, because they become frustrated when they see that the kids are often faster and more efficient at serving the homeless than they are. These self-centered people are thinking of themselves instead of the unfortunate people they are supposed to be helping. Many people often arrive too late to help set up the event, and leave before the difficult job of cleaning up begins at the end of the day. Seeing this, the kids conclude that these "helpers" come only to tell others that they have "done their share." Helping others seems to be the last thing on their minds. It's harsh criticism, but such hypocrisy is a good thing for young children to observe. Fortunately, most people serving at homeless shelters possess an inspiring generosity of spirit. Kids can observe the stark difference between true altruism in the many and seemingly generous behavior that sometimes masks selfishness beneath the surface in a few. It motivates a child to do the right thing for the right reasons.

## When Selfishness Is Creepy

*All About Eve*, which won the Oscar for best picture of the year in 1950, features Anne Baxter as Eve, a scheming young woman. She pretends to admire Margo, a brilliant but aging actress played by the remarkable Bette Davis, but the admiration is all an act. Eve manipulates everyone and everything to sabotage Margo and take over her life. Unfortunately, this doesn't just happen in Hollywood movies.

Several years ago, some of my former students were befriended by Susan, a talented young musician. These kids were part of the Saturday morning college preparatory classes. They raved about Susan's character and kindness. The Saturday class is made up almost entirely of former students, and it is rare to let anyone else in, but Susan was an exception. Her sweetness and seeming appreciation for the opportunity to learn won us all over. She spent about three months studying, and signed on to go to the Oregon Shakespeare Festival the following summer.

But it turned out that Susan had never planned to go to the festival. One of the only drawbacks to the fantastic reputation that the kids of Room 56 have earned is the tendency of some people to want to ride on their coattails. In some ways, it is a tribute to their success, but it's not fun for the kids to feel used for their hard work. Susan, it turned out, used her association with the class to earn an audition to an elite music school, and then promptly disappeared. I was certainly frustrated, but that was nothing compared to the anger and hurt feelings of the students she had "befriended." Susan ended up winning a scholarship to the school, where she thrives today.

This brings up the hardest task facing parents. The sad truth is that selfish people often get what they want. Perhaps this difficult real-world fact explains why we love fairy tales, where the good always come out on top and the bad suffer their just deserts.

But life is not a fairy tale, and to teach children to behave selflessly when the Eves and Susans of the world get what they want is a tough sell. That's why children need to understand what Eve and Susan lose in getting what they want—the trust and respect of friends, to start, but also the chance to make a real difference in the lives of others. Children need to understand that a selfish life produces a narrow view of what the world has to offer, a view that barely gets beneath the surface to where so much of what makes life interesting lurks. Extraordinary children think of others because they know that getting what they want isn't always the point. Parents can help them see the bigger picture.

## The Philanthropic Backpack

Putting money in the collection plate at church or feeding the homeless on Thanksgiving are both acts of kindness, but the old cliché is still true: charity begins at home. When kids build a home life that rejects selfishness, they begin to understand that kindness and generosity aren't reserved for special occasions. This is the sentiment behind satirist and songwriter Tom Lehrer's brilliant tweaking of National Brotherhood Week when he croons, "be grateful that it doesn't last all year." A generosity of spirit cannot be momentary. It must be a way of life.

*Food for Thought*

Children need to be a part of the preparation of dinner. Too often, kids today are called to the table—usually from in front of a television set—only when the meal is ready. Food is placed in front of them. They eat and rush off before they have even swallowed their last mouthful, eager to return to the day's scheduled programming.

When kids regularly help prepare the meal or set the table, they learn to share with others and practice unselfish behavior each evening rather than on holidays only.

There is a simple game my class plays at the end of every day that visitors love to observe. You can play the same game with your children at the dinner table. It requires no preparation and is a valuable addition to the lesson plans you use to teach your children unselfishness. In our class we call it "the compliment game."

George Harrison inspired people everywhere when he wrote "When you've seen beyond yourself you may find peace of mind waiting there," and I was certainly one of the converted. Over the years, I've thought about how we can get children to see beyond themselves.

In most classrooms, the day's end consists of cleaning the room and the review of homework assignments. Those are certainly important activities, but I make sure they are finished with about five minutes to go. Then we start our game. Children voluntarily raise their hands to praise someone in the class or in their lives. A typical day might include the following comments:

DENNIS: I'd like to thank Mike. Today, when I was making my string art project, he stopped doing his own design and helped me hammer my nails when I was having trouble.

ELSA: I'd like to compliment Mr. Vasquez. He helped me find the book I needed in the library today. He's really a nice librarian.

RIA:      I'd like to compliment Kevin. I think he is doing
           much better in school. I remember in fourth
           grade he got in trouble for never doing his home-
           work. He always gets things done now. He's a
           much better student.
(The rest of the kids applaud.)


It's such a nice way to end the day. At the dinner table, interested parents often ask their children to talk about their day and
how they are doing in school. This is a useful activity, but it can
be made even better by adding this compliment-giving compo-
nent. Night after night, for a few minutes a child needs to stop
and consider all the good people in the world who made his day a
bit better, from classmates to family members to teachers to anonymous strangers. Those five minutes a night can lead to a lifetime
of selfless behavior. To quote Wally Lamb, "I know this much is
true": with the compliment game children will see beyond themselves tomorrow, and tomorrow, and tomorrow.


*Please, Mr. Postman*

From the moment kids can hold a pencil, written thank-you cards
are a must. With the popularity of e-mail and text messaging on
the rise, sincere expressions of gratitude to others are becoming a
thing of the past. When a youngster acknowledges another person's kindness in writing, he takes the time to think about the
birthday gift or the gift of time someone has given. Selfish children do not think beyond the gift itself to see that the present
they unwrapped was the result of planning, time sacrificed, and
money spent by another person. Writing down an appreciation

for this process makes a lasting impression on child and gift giver alike.

Thank-you cards do not have to come from a store. They should, however, be neatly written and presented. Such care tells the giver that the recipient is truly appreciative. Young recipients of gifts will be motivated to become more considerate when they take the time to acknowledge the generosity of others.

### Community Chest (without a Monopoly Board)

Good schools often have a community service requirement. To fulfill this requirement, kids must help out at a senior center or day-care facility and have their hours of service witnessed and recorded by an adult. These are worthy activities, but unless students really understand the importance of service they will fulfill the task not to make the world better but only to improve their report card.

If parents want their children to accept JFK's challenge, they must set the example. It's a great idea to tackle community service as a whole family. Pick a cause that improves the community. It might be working at a homeless shelter one night a week or volunteering to clean up graffiti. If your schedule allows for it, spending a couple of weeks a year working for Habitat for Humanity is another great option. Whatever the cause, if a family makes helping others a part of their lives, it will be assimilated into the children's thinking. It will no longer be perceived as a mere assignment to complete, but as integral a part of life as eating or breathing.

*Reel Altruism*

The 1963 movie *Lilies of the Field,* starring Sidney Poitier, is a marvelous choice for a family film night. Poitier plays Homer Smith, a handyman who is cajoled into building a chapel for some of the most stubborn nuns this side of *The Sound of Music.* As Homer begins construction, he refuses to let the community help. It has to be his work alone. As the film progresses, Smith learns that though he is "helping" others, selfishness and pride are preventing him from seeing the bigger picture. Homer learns to accept the kindness of strangers, and his personal growth coupled with the generosity of the community results in a reward far greater than his own individual achievement.

And when your child is ready to go to the head of the class, make sure *Casablanca* is part of the final exam in selflessness. The iconic World War II masterpiece is a staple in Room 56 on Valentine's Day, but the film's lessons are evergreen. Boys and girls of all ages fall in love with Humphrey Bogart's tough-guy nightclub owner, Rick Blaine, who says of himself, "I stick my neck out for nobody." Like Prince Hal in *Henry IV,* his outward shallowness conceals a deep and hidden reservoir of decency and honor.

In case you are one of the few people on the planet who have not had the pleasure of watching this classic film, let me fill you in on the basics. The movie centers on three desperate people in Casablanca, Morocco, during the 1940s as Nazis prepare to occupy the city. Great character actors such as Claude Rains and Peter Lorre make every scene memorable. The script is brilliant, and practically every line has been memorized by millions of devoted followers.

Rick has two letters of transport that will allow their owners to escape Casablanca and flee to America. He and Paul Henreid's heroic rebel, Victor Laszlo, both love Ilsa, beautifully played by Ingrid Bergman. It appears Bogart will turn in Victor to the Nazis, and use the letters to escape with the woman he loves. But in the memorable ending, he stays behind and sends Ilsa off with Victor. As they part, he tells her: "Ilsa, I'm no good at being noble, but it doesn't take much to see the problems of three little people don't amount to a hill of beans in this crazy world. Someday you'll understand that."

It's an incredible act of sacrifice, one that has inspired viewers (and lots of weeping) for more than sixty years. *Casablanca*'s lessons of giving up oneself for the greater good are impossible to forget.

## Living by the Book

For young children, Shel Silverstein's masterpiece *The Giving Tree* is required reading. In the book, a little boy makes friends with a tree. At every stage of his life, the boy uses the tree for a variety of needs, from shade to building materials. Thoughtful kids often feel sad at the end for the tree, which has given everything to the person in the story. It's a perfect fable to send a child down a path that encourages a balance between giving and receiving.

Harper Lee's *To Kill a Mockingbird* is filled with so many astonishing quotes it rivals *Hamlet* as a source to be committed to memory. For the purposes of teaching a child to choose generosity over selfishness, take the time to discuss Scout's reflections of Boo Radley after her ordeal is over: "Neighbors bring food with death, flowers with sickness, and other things in between.

Boo was our neighbor. He gave us two soap dolls, a broken watch and chain, a pair of good-luck pennies, and our lives. But neighbors give in return. We never put back into the tree what we took out of it. We had given him nothing, and it made me sad."

Any person who takes the time to learn this passage will remember to put things back in the tree. When your child does that, you have accomplished a very difficult task. You have taught your kid President Lincoln's appeal that we seek out "the better angels of his nature." The world will be better and your child happier. It is worth all the conversations and struggles to get there.

## End of the Sixth

Things were looking up. The Dodgers had scratched out a couple of hits, followed by a home run from a player not known for power. In Twain's words, it was a thunderbolt out of a clear sky. The game was tied up, 5–5, with three innings to go. The kids were excited. Cesar, the healthiest eater of the bunch, wanted to know if I could afford to give him a few extra dollars to get some fruit being sold at a stand called The Healthy Plate.

In times past there had been many nights when I couldn't afford the extra treat. Teachers don't make a lot of money and the food at the ballpark is outrageously expensive. Tonight, though, I had plenty of extra money for the children. The month before, during spring break, I had received a visit from Joseph, the young man who had for years thought only of himself. He had spent his childhood reading the books and watching the films discussed above and spent more hours than he cared to remember listening to me ramble on about unselfishness. That day at the University of Pennsylvania, when I was weighed down by twenty shirts and pennants and he had asked to pile on more, I had given up trying to convince him.

But you never know when your efforts will finally take hold. During Joseph's winter and spring vacation breaks, the gifted young man had interned at a science laboratory and had performed exceptionally there. The lab had not planned to pay him, but was so impressed with his work that they gave him a thousand dollars, a huge sum for a kid expecting nothing.

The following day he cashed the check and took a bus one hundred miles from his boarding school to come back to Room 56. He gave all the money to me to use for the fifth graders.

Cesar enjoyed his fruit salad. And Joseph, like the Dodger outfielder, had hit one out of the park.

# Even Higher

## Top of the Seventh

The crowd was surprisingly quiet and thinning out. The Dodgers had rallied and tied the score, yet thousands of fans headed for the exits.

Fortunately, this included the men in front of us with their little boy. In a fitting farewell, he managed to poke one of the students with his flag one last time. With their view unobstructed and some mean people literally out of the picture, the kids anticipated an exciting end to their evening. Another relief pitcher had entered the game for the Dodgers, and the children were busy writing in his name and number on their score sheets.

The students had done a magnificent job at their first game. They cheered for the Dodgers, but respectfully applauded the Cardinals. They were well mannered and kept their areas clean. The young scholars had learned some of the nuances of the game while taking good care of one another. And the icing on the cake, the best thing of all, was that few people in the stadium had noticed them. In achieving this, they had demonstrated the most important character trait of all.

They were humble.

Humility is even more difficult to teach than selflessness for two reasons. First, all of us need and enjoy a pat on the back from time to time. It is natural to want others to acknowledge our accomplishments. The second obstacle on the road to acquiring humility is that our social order looks down upon it; often the most obnoxious, arrogant, and repugnant people are celebrated in our society. From athletics to entertainment to politics, we are bombarded with information about people who boast of their deeds. Winners taunt losers. It is no longer sufficient to be good at something; success must be punctuated by insulting and degrading others. Talk radio, the Internet, and thousands of television stations are filled with screaming people calling attention to themselves in hopes of gaining profit or fame, and usually both.

A youth group that had arrived at the game late was among the people heading for the exits. As they reached the top level of the stairway, their staff led them in a chant:

> We're the best
> We're the best
> We're the best of all the rest.

This chant was repeated about a dozen times. Frankly, I was not sure what criteria were being used to justify its conclusion. From their disinterested looks, I doubted that these kids could have told you what teams were playing or the score. Their seats were a mess of spilled drinks and trash.

I don't mean to sound harsh about these children. It's easy to judge, and converts are often too hard on those who have not yet seen the light. I was once a young teacher who worried about being acknowledged, so I recognize too well the danger signs and the necessity of overcoming the need for attention.

Older teachers will recognize the journey so many hardworking young instructors make. Novice teachers put in long hours, and the best mature into class leaders who communicate important lessons to students in environments often not conducive to teaching. When odds are overcome and something meaningful has been accomplished, it is completely understandable to desire that the world see what has been done and give its seal of approval.

I don't know of a better teacher in the world than Dave Crumbine, a charismatic and brilliant class leader in Houston, Texas. Nobody works harder, cares more, and has more genuine teaching talent than Dave. His students excel because of his inspirational diligence and sincere desire to help them. Entering his classroom makes any visitor want to be in the fifth grade again.

Dave loves to teach history, and actually takes his class to the Washington, D.C., area *twice* a year. He is fascinated by Thomas Jefferson, and an annual trip to Monticello is always a highlight of the school year. Thanks to Dave's doggedness, his kids know more about America's past than many adults do. It's marvelous to spend time with Dave's delightful students.

But even outstanding teachers have things to learn. In his youth, Dave would often tell his many friends and admirers that he wanted the docents at historic sights like Monticello to discover that his kids knew more history than they, the docents, did. It's understandable that Dave would feel that way, considering his enormous sacrifices and hard work. He was proud of his students, and was determined to show off their abilities to all whose paths they crossed.

But higher ground awaited, a place where it did not matter whether people knew his kids were great. When kids *are* great, that is the reward in itself. In time, Dave came to understand a crucial lesson: we should learn history for the love of the knowledge rather than the desire to impress others. Knowing this changed him; it made him a better teacher, and his kids better students. These days Dave and his kids are more brilliant than ever, and no one knows. They have reached that higher ground.

I've been down in the valley. As a new teacher in the early 1980s, I submitted a proposal to the Los Angeles Unified School District for a project that would help kids learn English by teaching them Shakespeare. No one believed in the project. I received polite rejections and condescending lectures. I was too young; the kids were not capable; no one cares about a dead white man. I heard every excuse imaginable to explain that the kids would never like Shakespeare.

I was a young man full of pride and ambition, so I had to prove everyone wrong. In doing so, I lost sight of the objectives of the proposed project. Rather than helping kids learn English, it became a chance for me to be able to say "I told you so." It is embarrassing to admit to such wrongheadedness, but that's the beauty of life: we can learn from our mistakes.

My insistence on showing off to the world the success of my young charges in learning Shakespeare reached its frenzied peak at The Old Globe theater in San Diego's Balboa Park. The theater consists of a beautiful complex of stages, and for several years the kids would come with me and spend lovely summer evenings watching Shakespeare.

Amid the theaters is a grassy area where people can relax and picnic before seeing a show. It's a lovely environment, even though performances are punctuated by background sounds coming from the San Diego Zoo. Rather than enter the theater right away after a picnic, I used to have the children do little performances on the lawn to demonstrate to the public that they were special.

My wife, Barbara, would cringe. She lectured me constantly that these small presentations were unnecessary. The people on the grass were not there to watch the kids. They had their own plans, and it didn't matter whether they liked the kids or not. Their approval would not help the kids learn English, mature, or have better lives. Of course she was right.

Once I listened to Barbara, the children's knowledge of Shakespearean performance became far superior to that of my classes in earlier years. All of my energy became focused on the kids rather than on what others might think. My discovery that proving oneself to others is a waste of time paid huge dividends in the children's growth.

These days, the children are asked to perform Shakespeare all over the world. The kids are happy to do so, and in the words of the Royal Shakespeare Company, "The Hobart Shakespeareans are the ultimate example of how and why Shakespeare should be performed. And it's so much fun to watch."

It's ironic that when I learned to stop trying to impress others, people became impressed! That's the beauty of teaching and practicing humility. Everyone wins. When I truly understood the importance of humility, I became a better role model for the students. After all, the first rule of parenting and teaching is to be the people we want the kids to be. After a recent performance by the kids at the Oregon Shakespeare Festival, an enthusisastic teacher wrote about her reactions to the show:

> As a young violin student, I was trained in a method called Suzuki. It focuses almost exclusively on listening, imitating, and mimicking, the idea being that students are able to quickly learn technique and then play songs right away. I guess I was pretty good at playing by ear because I rapidly advanced through the books and soon, I was playing difficult pieces at an early age. Later, much to my horror, I discovered that while I could play difficult compositions and make them sound okay, I really had no idea what I was doing. No one ever sat me down, held up a Mozart concerto and said, "Okay, you've heard this a million times, but what do you see?"
>
> But on this stage, there is much more than just the notes on a paper. I also see hours and hours of hard work, dedication and persistence. I see a group of kids who understand the value of staying the course instead of opting for a quick, ready out-of-the-box solution. I see children who perform for a group of thousands the exact same way they would perform for a group of two—the hallmark of a true musician. I see students who practice and are diligent, not because they seek attention or praise, but because it's who they have become. Their accomplishments are much more than what they've done and what they know, it's who they are.

This thoughtful teacher summarizes everything that is right and wrong with the process of learning. If the performance (or test at the end of the year) is all that counts, there is no joy and certainly no real understanding on the part of the student. Even well-meaning adults can lose sight of what really matters. When I learned to teach children to not be distracted by audiences, opening nights, and, most important of all, their own egos, the work itself took center stage. And when it did, brilliant and happy performers were born.

## Seventh-Inning Stretch

A two-run homer by one of the Cardinals' best players had put St. Louis up, 7–5. Things didn't look good for the Dodgers this evening. As the crowd rose to sing "Take Me Out to the Ball Game," the Cardinal superstar left the dugout to return to his defensive position. The men behind us began yelling at him. One man in particular was especially emphatic:

HECKLER: Fuck you! Fuck you! You suck! Go fuck yourself and I'll fuck your wife.
(laughter from his friends and some of the sur-
rounding fans)

RAFE: Hey, sir? [points to the children]

HECKLER: What the fuck's *your* problem?

RAFE: No problem, but they're only ten. Can we tone
it down a bit?

HECKLER: Fuck you too! Go fuck yourself! What the fuck
you gonna do about it?

> (raises his beer with the veiled threat of spilling
> it on all of us)

RAFE:     Nothing. Sorry to have bothered you, sir.

Albert Einstein defined *insanity* as doing the same thing over and over again and expecting different results. Having foolishly attempted to have the group in front of us curb their child's behavior, I repeated the mistake by asking someone else to clean up his language. I received similar rewards for both efforts. The funniest—or perhaps saddest—thing of all was that after listening to the men for a while the children discovered that two of them were teachers. Ouch!

The kids asked if I could take them to the bathroom, which was fine with me as I had to go as well. In my youth, I could drink several bottles of water or Coke and never leave my seat. Times have changed.

For me as for most people, bathroom time is usually a private moment, so I was startled when the man in the next urinal started a conversation. It turned out to be one of the men seated behind us whose friend had cursed me when I asked him to clean up his language. The man in the bathroom had recognized the kids from the PBS documentary *The Hobart Shakespeareans*, which had been shown during one of his school's staff meetings. He wanted to apologize. He offered me a handshake, but I thought it might be better to wash our hands first. Outside the bathroom, we had a nice chat:

TEACHER:  Hey, man, sorry about what happened with my
              friend before. He was just playing around, you
              know? He was just busting your balls a little,
              y'know?

RAFE:        No worries. Gotta get back to the kids, though. You understand.

TEACHER:     Can I ask you a question?

RAFE:        Of course. Fire away.

TEACHER:     Why you doin' this?

RAFE:        Doin' what?

TEACHER:     You know. Working all the time. Taking the kids all over.

RAFE:        Well, I enjoy it. Teaching kids is great, isn't it?

TEACHER:     Yeah, I love it. You makin' a lot of money?

RAFE:        Not really.

TEACHER:     Well, you write books and I saw you on television. You could retire, right?

RAFE:        Uh . . .

TEACHER:     Come on, there's no press around. Just between us. Why are you still doin' it?

RAFE:        I just really like it.

TEACHER:     Come on . . .

RAFE:        Okay, but just between us, right?

TEACHER:     Right!

RAFE:        My wife wants a new kitchen. If I can get some more money from books or a movie, she can get the new kitchen. But that's just between us, okay?

TEACHER:     I knew it! Thanks, man. Have fun.

RAFE:        You too.

There was a time when I would have desperately tried to explain to this guy that I was only trying to do the best job I could as a teacher. Much energy would have been expended on my part justifying my existence and trying to impress him with the abilities and accomplishments of my students.

But telling him I was still teaching because my wife needed a new kitchen made him feel better. He didn't have to know about Cesar's accomplishments or Yo Yo's singing. Years earlier, I would have tried to show him the results of going the extra mile, and justifying how ordinary children can become truly special. I am, I hope, a little wiser now in realizing that trying to prove anything to the world is a waste of everyone's time. These days, when anyone asks me why I would spend so many hours with the kids and the truth doesn't seem to satisfy them, I always answer that it's because my wife needs a new kitchen. And everyone walks away happy.

## Bottom of the Seventh

As the kids got ready to watch the last of the seventh inning, Cesar was practicing some of his speeches from *As You Like It.* He had been coached by Felix, a former student, two years his senior. Felix was one of the finest students—and people—ever to pass through Room 56, yet his unassuming personality and quiet strength helped him remain humble. Though he never asked for admiration, the younger students had placed him on a very high pedestal.

Felix was intelligent and very talented, particularly as a comic actor. He was extremely good-looking, with flowing hair that hung down to his shoulders, and his timing onstage was excellent. Cesar had received quite a lot of acting help from this mentor. All the kids respected Felix for remaining a model of humility when enormous talent could have made him insufferable. Having been exposed to such modesty, the kids were inspired to follow in Felix's footsteps. He quietly set a standard of kindness and sensitivity. When he would return from middle school on a day off to help out in the class, Felix always chose the hardest jobs. He was the first kid to clean up a messy spill, and the one who would spend an extra twenty minutes with a struggling student deemed "unteachable" by others.

It was no surprise that during this current year, the most troubled students in class were always taken under Cesar's wing. After all, the wondrous Felix had shown him the way.

## The Unassuming Backpack

The temptation to prove oneself in the eyes of others too often gets the best of us. Many parents put bumper stickers on their cars advertising the news that their child is an honor student. It may be true but it is not necessary to boast about it. It's *fantastic* that a child is doing well, but that should be the reward in itself. Using Kohlberg's levels as a moral framework, we should want our kids to live at level 6. Students should not strive to be first-rate thinkers in order to impress neighbors. Once the bumper sticker has been peeled off, it's time to reinforce the importance of modesty by exposing children to extraordinary people who are even more special because of their reserve.

### No, Thank You, Holidays

At the end of Charles Dickens's *A Christmas Carol,* Ebenezer Scrooge promises to keep Christmas all year long for the rest of his life. He begins by anonymously sending a prized turkey to his poor clerk, Bob Cratchit, whom he has treated badly. It's a wonderful gesture, made all the better by his keeping the gift anonymous. Similarly, in episodes of the old TV series *The Lone Ranger*, the masked hero would perform good deeds and then quickly ride away, leaving the beneficiaries to say, "And we didn't even get a chance to thank him." It's a sentiment worth instilling in your child, and holidays provide an opportunity to do so.

It's wonderful when families donate time to the local homeless shelter on Thanksgiving and Christmas, but, like Scrooge, they would soar even higher if this spirit was maintained year-round. One idea is to quietly perform good deeds on other holidays throughout the year. I have seen both classrooms and families celebrate Arbor Day by planting trees with a local environmental group. One class I visited spends the morning of Memorial Day anonymously sending gift baskets to veterans. A colleague of mine participates in a ten-kilometer walk every Independence Day, raising funds for muscular dystrophy research.

By making each holiday a time when we improve the world without drawing attention to ourselves, we can teach our children the value of humility. Each holiday presents an opportunity for a different lesson: before the Labor Day picnic or barbecue, for instance, it would be nice to prepare a meal for someone who does not have the good health or finances to manage it alone. There are many organizations doing all sorts of good deeds quietly, avoiding the press or any credit for their work. They believe that charity is best done humbly. By using holidays to make the world a little better, your child will know this too.

## Humility That's Out of This World

One film that can be used to frame all the lessons and conversations you plan to have with your kid about humility is *The Right Stuff* (1983). This movie was a box office failure, but it is brilliant nonetheless, and required viewing in Room 56. The film contains some salty language and is not for very young children, but it is great entertainment that features excellent lessons in history and character. It's a wonderful supplement for any parent trying to teach a child about "the right stuff." It is well and good for our children to reach the stuff that dreams are made on. Young people who pursue their dreams passionately with diligence and honor soar. Once in the clouds, however, it is essential for kids to realize they are very small, part of a much larger universe where their achievements need to be understood in the context of all who made their success possible.

One running gag in the film centers on Gordon Cooper, a young hot dog of a pilot drowning in arrogance and played superbly by Dennis Quaid. Several times in the film, he asks anyone who is listening, "Who's the best pilot you ever saw?" After a pregnant pause, he breaks into a sly grin and answers his own question: "You're looking at him."

The events of the movie change Cooper's outlook. As the film closes, the press surrounds him just before he is to go into space. They ask him his favorite question: "Who's the best pilot you ever saw?" Cooper grins and prepares to give his stock answer, but the personal growth he has experienced compels him to give an honest answer. He tries to tell the press the truth. There are countless great pilots, he explains, and many of them have died in the line of duty and remain unknown. He goes on to attempt to mention Chuck Yeager, the man who broke the sound barrier and had "the right stuff."

But no one is listening. The press does not want to hear the truth. They ignore Cooper, and when he realizes no one is paying attention, the hot dog returns to his familiar response: "You're looking at him." The press eats it up.

It's a complete encapsulation of the challenge facing parents, teachers, and students. Learning humility is difficult, especially when one realizes that most of our society is more interested in boasting and bragging. Hopefully understanding this will steel the resolve of our children in their quest to humbly discover the right stuff.


*A Modest Reading List*

Once your child has humility on his radar screen, he will begin to notice it in many of literature's great characters. Here are a few reading suggestions that can help humility remain in a kid's heart and mind.

Those seeking lessons on how to be humble often arrive at Bible tales and other religious stories. Richard Ungar's *Even Higher* is a Jewish folktale that makes perfect reading for young children. The author adapts a fabulous tale by I. L. Peretz about a Jewish town whose mysterious rabbi disappears every week just as the people are about to say prayers. All sorts of rumors circulate about the rabbi's whereabouts. While some of the towns-people spread sordid tales, others believe he ascends to open the gates of heaven so the prayers of his people will be heard.

A child decides to uncover the secret, and he sneaks into the rabbi's house and hides under the bed. On the Sabbath, the boy is shocked to see the religious leader secretly putting on peasant clothes and sneaking out of the village to the forest. There, this "peasant" chops wood for an old woman, kindles her fire, and says the prayers she is too sick to recite herself. When the boy returns to the village, he decides to become a disciple of this humble man, whose good deeds go unknown even to the recipients. When the townspeople ask the child if the rabbi goes to heaven, the boy responds, "Even higher."

It's especially important to discuss the issue of humility during adolescence, when children are most susceptible to societal and peer pressure to make a statement about their accomplishments. Middle school students are ready to be guided through John Knowles's classic, *A Separate Peace*. They should pay close attention during chapter 3, in which Phineas, a world-class athlete at the Devon School, is swimming with his friend Gene. No one else is around when Phineas discovers to his dismay that the school swimming record is not held by a member of their class. Though he has no formal swimming training, Phineas mounts a starting block, dives into the water, and, with Gene timing him, breaks the school record. Gene is struck dumb by the significance of such an accomplishment, and bemoans the facts that there were no witnesses and that he is not an official timekeeper. He expresses his desire to call the school newspaper and have Phineas repeat the feat the next day.

But Finny will have none of it. He wanted to know only if he could break the record, and that is enough for him. Gene is overwhelmed by the magnificence of this kind of thinking. Hopefully, your child will be as well. Reaching excellence is something special. Announcing it to the world is not.

Follow up with *To Kill a Mockingbird*. This is an important work to read when combating the misunderstanding that humility means quietude and weakness. The character Atticus Finch will help a child understand that to be modest actually takes great strength. In chapter 10, Finch's children, Jem and Scout, are embarrassed by their father, believing he is just an old man who can't do anything. They are not reassured when their neighbor, Miss Maudie, speaks up for him and says, "You'd be surprised."

Their eyes are opened when a mad dog comes to the streets of their town. As the townspeople cower in fear behind closed doors, Sheriff Tate hands Atticus a rifle to kill the dangerous animal. The modest lawyer fells the dog with one bullet, and Jem and Scout discover that their father is the best shot in the county. When Scout excitedly plans to tell all the kids at school about her father's marksmanship, her older brother dissuades her. Jem has realized that humility may be hard to achieve, but that it is a sign of strength and not weakness. He comes to know his father is a true gentleman, and wants to grow up to be like him.

Once a child has stood in Jem's shoes, he is ready for the next lesson. Charles Dickens's *Great Expectations* is a difficult but brilliant novel that high school kids should tackle. The book's young protagonist, Pip, suffers a miserable childhood with his ill-tempered sister and her gentle husband, Joe Gargery. Pip lives in hope that his future will bring "great expectations." However, he is tormented throughout his youth by the beautiful and mysterious girl Estella and her even stranger guardian, Miss Havisham. As Pip dreams of the riches he will have one day, he is particularly embarrassed by his brother-in-law, who works in the forge and always tries his best. The blacksmith is neither educated nor well mannered, but Pip cannot recognize that Joe is the father figure he should emulate. As Joe works doggedly in the forge, Pip literally does not "see the light." While Pip blindly looks to riches and other material goods to find happiness, he foolishly ignores the quiet and unassuming blacksmith, in whose example he should find great wisdom and depth of character. Pip may not see the truth, but readers do, and it's a great lesson for your child to apply to his own life.

Dickens's critics have often disparaged the story's sad ending, but it is necessary to reinforce the theme. Pip's story should not have a happy ending because he never sees the obvious solution to his problems. His arrogance prevents him from achieving real happiness; developing an unassuming nature would have been the better choice. Through Pip's tragic tale children can learn that a humble existence is the most fulfilling kind.

Finally, Arthur Miller's play *Death of a Salesman* will contribute to a young person's understanding that humility is an essential virtue if one wishes to succeed. While reading the play, kids should study the character of Bernard, the nerdy neighbor, who is looked down upon by Willy Loman and his two sons. In the second act, Bernard has grown up to be a successful attorney with a fine family. He has a conversation with Willy in which he speaks modestly, but then must depart to attend to work. Once he is gone his father, Charley, tells Willy that Bernard is going to argue a case in front of the United States Supreme Court. "He never even mentioned it!" Willy exclaims in stunned wonder. "He doesn't have to," Charley explains to Willy. "He's going to DO it."

## End of the Seventh

The relief pitchers' fresh arms had fooled batters on both teams, and the score remained deadlocked at 7–5. The children continued to run through some lines of Shakespeare, and laughed as Cesar emulated his mentor, Felix, in both diction and appearance. The day before, Felix, always familiar by his beautiful shoulder-length hair, had shown up in class completely bald. It was quite a fashion statement.

Now, as the kids practiced lines, Cesar wrapped a napkin over his head to cover his hair, causing his friends to laugh hysterically. They stopped laughing when I explained to them what Felix had told me. I had asked him about the shaved head, and he told me that one of his classmates was ill with cancer and about to undergo chemotherapy. Felix had decided to give his friend his hair. I asked him if this was a school project. "No," he replied simply, and skirted out the door to get home to do his chores.

The transition from laughter to dead seriousness was instant. The children sat in stunned silence, but it was obvious what they were thinking. They could perform Shakespeare and already had test scores that would one day be good enough for a top university. They had mastered the mathematics of scoring a baseball game. Their manners were impeccable.

But one day they would follow Felix. He had gone even higher.

# School Daze

During the break before the eighth, the crowd laughed at the entertainment provided courtesy of the huge Diamond Vision screen. Cameras were turned on couples in the crowd who cooperated by kissing, to the delight of the general public.

The children were not interested in watching strangers kiss. They had matters of greater consequence on their minds. It was the end of May, and their elementary education would end in less than a month. Middle school beckoned.

There was a time when children automatically attended their neighborhood public school. The thought of going anywhere else wasn't even considered. Children from the same neighborhood went to elementary, middle, and high school together, and that was that.

Times have changed. The fifth graders with me do not plan to go to their local middle school. The standards at this school are shockingly low, which has in turn produced a sense of fatigue among its faculty. This is a sad but understandable chain of events. Degrading societal values and poverty have created school environments where kids are increasingly rude and apathetic. That apathy drains class leaders of the enthusiasm and joy that should be a part of teaching. As the teachers surrender, the kids grow even more unruly. It is a vicious downward spiral, and concerned kids and parents often seek out alternative schools that might provide a safer haven.

Selecting a college is nothing new, but for many families today the quest for a decent education begins with choosing an elementary school. Some families have gone one step further and given up looking altogether, opting instead for homeschooling. There is no easy solution to the problem of finding the ideal situation. Keeping kids at home is the answer for some, but others reject this in favor of a social academic environment at a private school or an alternative public institution, like a charter or magnet school. Whatever their decision, all concerned parents share one motivating factor: they don't want their budding scholars trapped in a school where they are bored, scared, and miserable.

This chapter contains suggestions for parents who share these concerns and are searching for that special place where their child can flourish.


## Mind the Gap

The hunt for a better situation for your child might lead you to a charter or private school. Some of these are outstanding centers of education while others are mediocre. Here's one important thing to remember: by definition, these schools are asking you to voluntarily select them as the place that will give your child the best education possible. They are saying, "Send us your kid. We can do a better job than the local public school." And sometimes when a parent justifiably asks for evidence that an institution can deliver on its promise, a credibility gap appears.

When investigating the potential of private or charter schools, parents need to ask the right questions, ones that will produce a true picture of a school's academic environment. The obvious question "What makes your school better?" is usually answered by presenting a litany of impressive test scores. Standardized testing has become the dominant talking point of charter schools, particularly in "proving" that they are doing a better job than other schools in the system. Assessments *do* matter, but they are not *all* that matters. Your child is going to spend thousands of hours at the school you select; given this, your search criteria need to go far beyond test scores. The best schools are focused on helping children grow and achieve in ways that cannot be measured on standardized tests. Test scores speak not to means, but to ends. They look good on a school's publicity brochure but in reality tell a small part of the story.

For example, the previous summer I had taken some kids to a Dodgers game on a Sunday afternoon. It was uncomfortably hot, with temperatures approaching three digits. The students had all brought hats with towels attached to protect their necks, and sunscreen to shelter their faces. As we walked through the parking lot we saw a school group of almost fifty kids standing and baking uncomfortably on the asphalt. These kids were from a well-known charter school, whose "accomplishments" had been touted nationally. They were easily recognizable, as all the students wore shirts with the school's name on it. The kids were a bit grumpy, as they were standing in the sunlight sweating profusely while a group of teachers stood apart having a rather heated (sorry) discussion. Several teachers felt it necessary that the kids keep their shirts tucked in because of the impression it would make on the public. Others disagreed. The discussion must have lasted at least thirty minutes because we did not see the group enter the stadium until the second inning. The shirts were tucked in, and the children looked miserable. They sat near us during the game, but it was clear that most of these kids were unprepared. They threw food at one another and barely watched the action. The entire group left after the sixth inning, shirts still tucked in.

If a school's teaching staff is more interested in how the kids *look* at a baseball game than having them learn about the game itself, it might not be the right place for your child. The best place for a child to achieve excellence is at a school where the culture is concerned more with how things *are* than with how they *look*.

## One Size Does Not Fit All

Even excellent schools vary to a great degree in their beliefs about classroom environment. There are great schools with well-deserved exceptional reputations, but such places still might not be the best choice for your youngster. Finding the right school involves not only making sure that the institution meets high standards of excellence but also seeking out a comfortable fit for your child, especially if this means ensuring a diverse campus experience.

Samantha and Maria, two of my former students, were courted by a top prep school and offered scholarships to attend from sixth through twelfth grade. Their families were ecstatic. These girls had landed spots at a prestigious academy whose graduates attended the finest universities in the nation. It seemed to be a dream come true.

From an academic standpoint, the school's credentials were unimpeachable. The curriculum was fantastic and so were many of the teachers. The majority of the staff was knowledgeable, hard-working, and attentive. The reading lists used in both English and history were impressive, ranging from the classics to newer multi-cultural selections.

Samantha and Maria, both Latina girls from working-class backgrounds, understood the tough road in front of them. They were about to attend a challenging school filled predominantly with white children from wealthy families. Being successful would require working hard and adjusting to a new, unfamiliar environment.

Within weeks the girls had established themselves as two of the best students in their class. But they were miserable. Eleven years old at the time, both girls were humble and shy. They dressed modestly and looked and acted their age, but most of their peers at the school did not. Samantha and Maria had classmates who looked like they were going on seventeen and eighteen. These girls wore revealing clothing that made Samantha and Maria feel uneasy. Fitting in turned out to be more difficult than they had expected. It felt to them like life in the fast lane, surrounded by girls who were far more social than they cared to be at this point in their lives.

The girls survived two years there, minding their parents' pleas to endure and give the new situation time to become comfortable. It never did. Both girls decided to leave the school after finishing seventh grade. A different private school was eager to enroll them. This new preparatory academy had a very different social atmosphere—the kids all wore simple clothing and little makeup. It also had a different but equally compelling curriculum. At this new school, the girls continued to thrive academically, but they were much happier. The comfortable fit turned out to matter most.

## Middle of the Eighth

The men sitting behind us got up to leave, and I could feel the children exhale a quiet sigh of relief. The man from the bathroom gave me a pat on the shoulder while one of his friends shot me a dirty look. Seriously, it shouldn't be this hard to take a group of kids to a ball game.

This leads to an important discussion. As stadiums are often not family-friendly, many people have drawn the reasonable conclusion not to take their children. Why bring kids to an event where drunken hecklers and other misfits create an atmosphere unfit for children? Is it worth braving this kind of behavior to allow the kids to experience what could potentially be a night of learning and fun at the ballpark?

A good answer to this question comes from Otto Frank via a woman named Cara. Otto Frank was Anne Frank's father. During World War II, he survived a concentration camp and returned home to Amsterdam to learn that his wife and two children had been killed by the Nazis. After Anne's diary was published, Mr. Frank became a father figure to children all over the world. Cara was one of thousands who wrote to him, and over the years they developed a regular correspondence.

The political and social upheaval in the United States in the 1960s had a huge effect on Cara, and after Robert Kennedy had been assassinated in Los Angeles, she wrote a letter to Otto expressing her sadness. In it, she said she would never start a family, as life seemed too violent and awful to ever bring kids into the world.

In response, she received the only angry letter he ever wrote her. Mr. Frank scolded Cara, saying that he knew well the pain and anguish life can have in store. He stated categorically that Cara must have children, and raise them to be fine people. That, he counseled, was how the world could be changed.

Cara heeded his advice and went on to raise a beautiful family. One day she visited my class and told us the story of Otto Frank's letter. This message resonated with me, and I saw that its lesson applied not just to children we may bring into the world but also to those who are already here. We can never shield our kids completely from unpleasantness, but we can use the example of what's wrong in the world to show them how to make things right. That's why I take children to a game even when I know there's a good chance we'll be surrounded by boors. We have to be the change.

## Bottom of the Eighth

Baseball is a beautiful game. There is very little hidden beneath the surface of what needs to be accomplished. Sure, the complexities of different pitches and strategies may be beyond the grasp of the casual observer, but the task facing the Dodgers was simple to comprehend. They were two runs down and needed to score if they were going to win the game. If they were not able to accomplish this, they would lose. There is a beauty and even a comfort in this simplicity.

Unfortunately, choosing the right school for your child can be anything but simple. There are many factors to consider, and your child's happiness cannot be recorded like a baseball statistic on a series of columns to be tabulated at the end of the day. Adding to the confusion is that while there are fabulous schools available, there are others that shine only on the surface. As with wax fruit, the shine can conceal a lack of substance beneath. What you see is not always what you get.

## Beware of Spin Doctors

Most alternative schools have days when parents are invited to tour their campus. Such days are necessary but are often little more than dog-and-pony shows. The day is set up specifically to impress, but the image it portrays is often a far cry from the school's everyday reality. Remember the musings of Holden Caulfield in J. D. Salinger's *The Catcher in the Rye*. Holden points out that his school, Pencey Prep, serves the students steak every Saturday night. He is sure this is because parents visit on Sundays, so when they ask their kid what he had for dinner the previous night, the student can answer, "Steak."

Some schools today even hire media consultants to improve their image in hopes of attracting potential customers. My principal and mentor, Mercedes Santoyo, heard about this and laughed. "Any school that would hire a PR person," she mused, "must *need* one."

## On the Road Again . . . Not So Fast

Taking kids on the road is essential for a complete education. A good school will do a fantastic job of exposing kids to environments beyond the campus, whether that means field trips to historic sites or visits to colleges for students approaching the application phase. Parents need to be sure that their children are properly supervised during these trips. On multiday excursions, travel companies are often hired to take the kids around to make things easier for the teachers. These organizations should be as vigilant as a parent would be, but this doesn't always happen. Every year children are injured or killed on school trips. Acts of God can't be accounted for, but many tragedies could be avoided with better supervision. When choosing a school that plans off-campus trips, find out who will be with the kids twenty-four hours a day.

Many preparatory academies offer college trips for their high-school-age students, and this is a great thing. Top scholars need to get out of their comfort zones and see the possibilities. However, a trip is only as good as the staff that runs it. There is a famous prep school in California whose press liaison touts its annual spring college trip, and boasts about the elite universities the kids visit. The future seems bright when the local paper celebrates young people hitting the road to discover great schools like Swarthmore and Smith.

Two of my former students went on such a trip, and when they returned they gave a completely different account from what was reported in the press. The story in the newspaper described the trip as meticulously organized, with young scholars supervised and mentored by an outstanding group of chaperones at all times.

According to the kids, they were not well cared for. There was one morning when they woke up at four o'clock in Chicago to catch a flight to New York, then deplaned and scrambled to get on a bus that was to take them to Poughkeepsie. The group had an appointment at Vassar later that day. The kids were starving—they had been given no breakfast or lunch. They complained to the trip leaders, who replied that eating was not important. Eating, they were told, could be done anytime, but seeing these colleges was why they were on the road. The kids went almost fourteen hours before they had a bite. After the tour of Vassar, they were put right back on the bus for a return trip to New York City. Upon arriving, the kids were told they had to find dinner on their own, and they were essentially let loose in the Big Apple with no chaperones. It sounds incredible, but it's true. Allowing high school juniors who had never been to New York to wander around the city by themselves—does anyone think this is a good idea?

When visiting schools that will take your child on the road, make sure you ask the most important question: Who will be caring for my kid? That is the biggest issue.

This college trip is a startling example of neglect. The trip's leaders were fortunate that the worst consequence was hunger. If a school puts forth its travel opportunities as a selling point, don't worry so much about the itinerary. Any good school will have a range of interesting destinations, but the best schools will go the extra mile to make sure children can enjoy the experience safely.

## Lies, Damn Lies, and College

Colleges and universities are guilty of the same credibility gap that plagues some private middle and high schools. Parents and their college-bound kids must be cautious when evaluating potential institutions. It's not as simple as looking at the list of best colleges in *U.S. News & World Report*. Little Ye Rim, the burgeoning photographer, had the right idea—get closer.

Helen was a jewel of a student. She was lovely and extraordinarily tuned in to the feelings of others. She grew up without a father, and faced the usual family dramas, but she never lost her focus. Helen was gold and the colleges knew it, which put her in the enviable position of having many options when it came to selecting a good school. One East Coast college was the most attractive to her because it offered a full scholarship. She would get free room and board in addition to an outstanding education.

In a city as diverse as Los Angeles, Helen never felt uncomfortable as a minority student, but she was a little hesitant to go to a school three thousand miles from home without seeing it herself. During spring break, she flew east and was met at the airport by a group of six minority students. They persuaded Helen that the school was honest in saying it had made great strides in diversity. As a young woman of color, this helped make her feel at home. They took Helen around the campus (which was practically empty over the break) and she decided this school would be the ideal place for her.

During freshman year, however, Helen discovered the truth: the kids who gave her the tour were the only minorities on campus! She couldn't help but feel deceived, and had a tough time getting comfortable. It was a difficult period of adjustment, and she cried often during her first year. She toughed it out, though, and graduated with honors. Looking back, she had a good college experience, but most likely would have been happier at a different, more diverse school. When I flew out for her graduation ceremonies, I asked how I could find her.

"Just look across the campus," she said, laughing. "You can't miss me."

## Sherlock Holmes First, the Backpack Later

*Look Before You Leap*

Returning to *The Catcher in the Rye,* we find that Holden has given us a warning about prep schools. He mentions an ad that he often sees in magazines touting the excellence of Pencey Prep:

> They advertise in about a thousand magazines, always showing some hot-shot guy on a horse jumping over a

fence. Like as if all you ever did at Pencey was play polo all the time. I never even once saw a horse anywhere near the place. And underneath the guy on the horse's picture, it always says: "Since 1888 we have been molding boys into splendid, clear-thinking young men."

Strictly for the birds. They don't do any damn more molding at Pencey than at any other school. And I didn't know anybody there that was splendid and clear-thinking and all. Maybe two guys. If that many. And they probably came to Pencey that way.

Holden might not be the most objective narrator, but he's hit on a problem when it comes to the question of image versus reality at private schools. Placing the right tools in your kid's backpack will help him accomplish great things, but it also helps to send him to a school that shares your philosophy. Heeding Holden's warning, here is a suggested list of things to consider when choosing an alternative school for your child:

- If the school touts only its test scores, you might consider looking for institutions that are proud of other accomplishments as well.
- Size matters. Sit in on classes and see if your child will be able to get individual attention.
- Try to visit the school on a day that hasn't been programmed for parents by the school. If possible, without being rude, come unannounced. The best schools are at their best every day, not just when they know guests are observing.
- Maintain a healthy cynicism when reading brochures

and annual reports. They are produced by people who are paid by the school.

- Look for gray hair among the teachers. Many new charter schools are often staffed by teachers who have less than three or four years' experience. If you were having an operation, would you prefer a first-year surgeon or one with ten years' practice? The best school staffs have a combination of rookies and old pros.

- Gather information about a school from many different sources. Talk to the school, of course, but also seek out parents and students at the school to get a good feel for the campus. A combination of happy teachers, students, and parents is a good indicator that you have found a special place.

- When it comes to college planning, avoid buying into the thinking that only a famous school will do. Do not accept "best college" lists as some sort of message from God. The people who make those lists do not know your child. Harvard might be considered the "best" university, but is it the best fit for your child? Fresno State might be a far better choice, depending on the individual student.

- When visiting colleges, try to go when regular classes are in session. Many trips arranged by schools often take place during spring break or summer, when the school is not operating in its usual way.

- Here are three statements you'll hear consistently on official college tours. Make sure the school can back them up with facts.

We believe in diversity.

Look around the campus to see if the belief has been translated into a reality. Sometimes you'll hear a tour guide talk up the school's diverse student body only to find that walking the campus feels more like wandering through Sweden.

There are very few fraternities and sororities on campus.

Whether your child wants to be involved or not, get the facts. There are some students who want to avoid the frat scene, only to discover that the college they have chosen was the inspiration for *Animal House.*

Our campus is completely safe.

Late in the tour, the guide often talks about the blue-light security system and campus escorts. Most campuses reflect the societal problems that are prevalent in the areas nearby, but if a campus is totally safe, why have security? Keep it real with your child and discuss this serious issue. Ask the admissions officer for crime statistics, and discuss these with your child to gauge his or her comfort level.

## Phi Beta Kappa Films

For parents who want to watch outstanding films about higher education with their college-bound son or daughter, it's not easy. There are many funny films about college life, but most of them focus on getting drunk, pregnant, arrested, or all three at once. Films like *Old School* are hilarious, but we're on a mission here. To quote the 1978 classic *Animal House*, it might be apropos when you are laughing to remember Dean Wormer's cautionary advice to the young frat pledge Flounder: "Fat, drunk, and stupid are no way to go through life, son."

After the laughter subsides, let us hope that our students can enjoy some silliness while staying focused on pursuing excellence. A good film to watch with your child is James Bridges's often overlooked 1973 drama, *The Paper Chase.* John Houseman is unforgettable as Professor Kingsfield, a Harvard Law professor. Timothy Bottoms plays Hart, who survives love, intensive study, peer pressure, and the terror of a brilliant professor. In the end, Hart wins the biggest victory of all: he discovers himself and remains true to his beliefs. May that be the goal for all children who hope to one day go to college.

## End of the Eighth

The Dodgers had gotten men on base but failed to score and still trailed by two runs. As the Cardinals came off the field the giant screen was filled with screeching animated cars, forcing the kids to huddle close together in order to hear one another. They returned to their discussion about middle school and their future.

As at the beginning of the game, we were practically alone in our section, Still, I was a bit down after tangling with several drunken fans over the last few innings. Let's face it: it's hard to raise children of honor and integrity in a world that too often seems shallow and mean-spirited. I needed to feel better about things, so with a break in the action I reached into my ever-present briefcase. Teachers grade papers any time there's a spare minute, even between innings of a baseball game. Rather than read essays the kids had written about *Lord of the Flies,* I pulled out a letter I had received earlier that day from Elizabeth, a former student who was now a senior at an Ivy League university.

She had thrived at college, and I was happy to hear that she was doing well. Some of what Elizabeth wrote is good encouragement for struggling parents who suffer days when they begin to wonder if all the work and worry is worth it. As Elizabeth reminds us, it always is.

> Hi Rafe!
>
> . . . It's finally my last year and I can't believe it. It's been a long road and it'll be long afterwards but I had a lot of fun during the progress I've made. I wouldn't be in the position if it weren't for you and Barbara supporting me since 4th grade. I think back to our math club, reading literature, SAT classes, and physical training. They helped me so much, even though, at the time, I only thought of doing those things because they were enjoyable. Now that I'm close to graduating and starting my own life, I get a little frightened about what's to come. I might have already had a breakdown if I had not learned the life lessons I learned in your class, from memorizing a guitar piece to the trips we took around the world.
>
> I guess I'm just reminiscing now, but seeing as how I can remember everything we did together, I wanted you to know that everything we did had a great impact on me.

Reading the letter was just the medicine I needed. When teaching a child for a year, never mind raising one for eighteen, it's important to remember that setbacks are inevitable. Trying to reason with the men around me had been a disaster. I'm not perfect, and you won't be either. But the most important thing, for the kids and for parents and teachers, is to stay focused. Letters like the one from Elizabeth help me do this.

I looked over at the kids, still discussing what school they would choose next year. I reminded them that whichever one they attended, it still boiled down to their own individual integrity. As Mark Twain said: "I never let school interfere with my education."

The children laughed heartily. I looked at their smiling faces and thought maybe, just maybe, in thirteen more years I would receive another wonderful letter.

# The Long Run

## Top of the Ninth

The Cardinals continued to lead, 7–5. What a long day it had been for all of us. It was hard to believe that sixteen hours earlier we had entered our classroom for some extra math study before school. These students had run an eight-minute mile, played baseball, practiced their knowledge of South American geography, studied integers, read *To Kill a Mockingbird,* reviewed D-day, worked with stream tables to re-create erosion, played classical and rock music, and rehearsed an entire Shakespeare play. All that can happen in the daylight hours before a night game at Dodger Stadium.

The kids watched the Cardinals and I watched the kids. The little ones were worried that the visiting team was about to increase its lead. I was worried about the students' futures. They are growing up in a school system that has decided to measure their success or failure by testing them to death at the end of each year. Rote memorization and meaningless multiple choice exams have replaced problem solving and decision making. The teaching of character has almost disappeared. With sadness, I thought about one of Oscar Wilde's brilliant observations: "We teach people how to remember, we never teach them how to grow."

We need to help children grow. There will be so many obstacles and pitfalls in the years to come. Fortunately, these children are well prepared to meet such challenges. They have been trained to understand the importance of time, been schooled in decision making, are unselfish and humble, are not television addicts but readers, set the highest of standards for themselves, and have the focus to sweep the streets like Shakespeare wrote poetry. Indeed, if the readiness is all, these kids are equipped to go.

Despite all these wondrous skills, success eludes many capable kids. There is always more room in their backpacks for another tool that can help them hurdle the barriers that will face them.

A final gift to give a child is an understanding of delayed gratification. In our fast-food society, we continue to speed things up in an effort to be more efficient. From instant coffee to three-day weight-loss programs, so much of what surrounds them makes it difficult for children to understand that producing good things requires time and patience.

The week before, I had gone to a store to purchase some board games for the students' annual trip to the Oregon Shakespeare Festival. The kids enjoy playing them while relaxing in their hotel rooms. All the usual suspects, such as Scrabble, were on the shopping list, but I laughed as I tried to purchase Monopoly—I could not find the original version. There were dozens of themed editions, ranging from Star Wars Monopoly to Beverly Hills Monopoly, but no plain old Monopoly. Most interesting of all was the fact that several of the adaptations advertised on the box that a "speed" feature had been added to allow the players to finish the game faster. What a bad message to send to children. Some things take time. It is possible that spending the extra time completing the original Monopoly game may prove to be a more satisfying experience than rushing things just to get a winner. Isn't the "process" supposed to be fun? Shouldn't it be about playing and not winning?

## Creating Two-Marshmallow Kids

Many books have cited Stanford University professor Walter Michel's fascinating observations on impulse control and delayed gratification. It's a story that is fun to share with young people. Children four years of age were taken into a room and given a marshmallow. Their guide told them he had to leave but would return soon. The kids were told they could eat the marshmallow, but if they waited for the man's return, they could have two.

The little ones were watched through a one-way mirror. Some of the kids grabbed their treat immediately, while others waited up to twenty minutes before the adult returned from his "errand." Fourteen years later a follow-up study found that the kids who waited for two marshmallows did substantially better on college entrance exams. Across the board, those who waited showed greater emotional intelligence in a wide range of characteristics that correlate with happiness and success. Describing this experiment to children is an effective way to introduce them to the idea that life is a long process, and what we do now can have an enormous effect on how our future will play out. We need to encourage our children to be "two-marshmallow kids."

It's a daunting task. We have a vision for what children can become, but they cannot possibly have the same dreams. A child who is ten years old isn't going to have a five-year plan. He has not lived long enough to appreciate the distance of that span of years. Yet the marshmallow example plants a seed, and we can nourish that seed through a series of activities that help a youngster see the wisdom of controlling his impulses and waiting for a greater reward.

## Middle of the Ninth

The Cardinals, however, were not waiting for anyone. They scored an insurance run in the top of the inning and led, 8–5. This prompted an exodus to the parking lot rivaling that of Moses and his people to the Red Sea. With a holiday weekend beginning, people wanted to beat the traffic and begin their barbecues and parties.

We stayed. Kids need to learn to finish what they start. Traffic and other matters would have to wait. The idea of staying the course and not rushing is all a part of delaying gratification. Besides, the Dodgers still had one more chance to tie or win the game. The odds were not in their favor, but the lesson in staying until the end of the game was far more important than the contest itself. Leaving would have been difficult in more ways than one: by this point, elephants could not have pulled the children from their seats. Completely absorbed in the spectacle and strategy of it all, they were having far too much fun to want to be anywhere else. Cesar hoped that the Dodgers would tie but not win the game. If they evened the score, he reasoned, there would be extra innings and we could stay even longer! Now, *there's* a two-marshmallow kid.

## Bottom of the Ninth

It turned out that waiting until the end of the game was a very good idea. Several Dodger pinch hitters came to bat, and the team rallied to score a run and load the bases. There were several delays as the Cardinals changed pitchers three times in the inning. The kids were able to see the stream of car taillights heading out of the parking lot, and remarked about all the people missing the best part of the game. As Graham Nash wrote in the song "Teach Your Children," it's thrilling to watch young people "become themselves" as they establish the "code that they can live by." Regarding delayed gratification, here are a few suggestions that might assist you in raising children who can see tomorrow, and tomorrow, and tomorrow.

## Marshmallows in a Backpack

### The Long Run

Kids need to learn that life is a marathon and not a sprint. To that end, it's healthy for children to be involved in long-term projects. Along the way to completing them, young people can grow to see that the process of the project is more important than the finished product. As Don Henley sang: "Who can go the distance? We'll find out in the long run."

## Puzzling but Fun

Jigsaw puzzles have disappeared from many children's lives, but it's always wonderful to find them in bedrooms or on family tables. They come in many levels of difficulty, making them useful for preschool children and high school kids alike. Difficult projects can take months to complete, and require sorting pieces, planning, and execution. There are also challenging three-dimensional puzzles with foam pieces that fit together to form famous buildings such as the United States Capitol or the Eiffel Tower. When the puzzle's content is carefully chosen, puzzle making can connect kids with those things in the world in addition to increasing their focus and patience. When families work together on them, it can lead to conversation and support that might be lacking in homes where the television usually blasts twenty-four hours a day.

There are dozens of easily accessible Web sites where you can search for a puzzle suitable for your child. Two good sites to find something fun and educational are www.puzzles.com and www.seriouspuzzles.com. There are puzzles that can help teach kids about history, art, or sports. Some brain teasers for the serious puzzle maker have more than twenty thousand pieces. Jigsaw puzzles can provide a satisfying antidote to Beverly Hills Monopoly.

## Encouraging Kids to Be Hookers

Sorry, just kidding. But another project that teaches delayed gratification is any endeavor involving yarn. Very few children know how to actually make things these days. Crafts like knitting and sewing are disappearing talents. Before kids learn these more difficult skills, making a latch hook rug is a good activity to help them have fun and cultivate a better understanding of waiting for something wonderful.

Our class gets its latch hook rugs from Michael's art-supply stores, but all kinds of kits can be found online. Excellent selections can be found at www.caron.com and www.marymaxim.com. Keep in mind that making rugs from a kit is not creating art. Beginners are simply following a pattern. But they are learning to work on a long-term project, stitch by stitch, which the Stanford marshmallow study indicates is a valuable skill for a child to possess. The rug kits have precut yarn, and our class uses sandwich bags to sort the thousands of strands by color. In this way children who make rugs are learning about color differentiation and organization while having fun.

Eventually, kids can design their own rugs by using their drawing skills or a computer to create an original pattern. Working with yarn can eventually lead to knitting and crocheting, and all of these projects encourage kids to rejoice in a finished product. They look forward to a light at the end of a tunnel (even if they have to crawl along ten thousand strands of yarn before they see it!).

## Kinder-Garden

Many schools and families already garden with their children, and for good reason. Gardens can teach children about the environment, nutrition, planning, and, of course, delaying gratification. It is the perfect project for kids growing up in a world where Monopoly has become a game of speed.

Several universities have studied the positive effects gardening can have on a child. Growing things is therapeutic and relaxing. With kids spending most of their waking hours in classrooms preparing for overemphasized tests, gardening can help them de-stress, have fun, and learn. A bonus here is that gardening connects kids to the natural world, something that is becoming increasingly rare as they spend more time in front of televisions. It also gives kids a frame-by-frame look at the wondrous process of nature, and provides an excellent metaphor for how real beauty and greatness are produced painstakingly and with great and constant effort. As the nation cries out for all of us to "Go Green," a garden can be the start of a way of life.

Gardening is also a great way to get involved with your child's school. There are first-rate teachers who would love to grow things with their students, but find that time constraints and disruptive children make the project impossible. With the help of some supportive parents, working on a garden can become a reality, with parents supervising the patch while the teacher works hard at a job that has become practically impossible on the best of days. With a class garden, those days get better for everyone involved.

A good place to get ideas when starting a garden project is www.kidsgardening.org.

## A Two-Marshmallow Book

It seems that Antoine de Saint-Exupéry's brilliant work *The Little Prince* is not read by as many children today as it was twenty or thirty years ago. Students in my earliest classes had all read it by the fifth grade. These days many students have not heard of it when I bring it up. It's a book that all families should read, as its marvelous lessons can benefit adults and children alike.

Chapter 23 has a fantastic passage that will inspire children to wait patiently for something greater than immediate happiness. The Little Prince is wandering in the desert when he meets a merchant. The man is selling pills that completely quench thirst, making the drinking of water obsolete. One pill a week will do the job. The tradesman explains that new studies have shown that a man can save fifty-three minutes a week by taking the pills.

The Little Prince contemplates this information and thinks to himself: "If I had fifty-three minutes to spend as I liked, I should walk at my leisure toward a spring of fresh water."

Wonderful!

## The Play's the Thing

Each year the kids in Room 56 perform an unabridged production of Shakespeare. And here's the joke: the play has less to do with Shakespeare than one might imagine. I love Shakespeare's plays, but they are merely a vehicle to teach children an even more important lesson. I am a Shakespeare fan, so his plays are the perfect tool for me to use, but any long-term project can be used to the same advantage.

The rehearsals are all about delayed gratification. The children spend a year producing the play, and that is by design. It does not *have* to take that long. The rehearsal schedule is intentionally planned this way to allow the kids to experience the process of growth, and to understand that the end product has far less value than the thousands of rehearsals that precede opening night. The students in Room 56 collectively spend about *fifty thousand hours* working on a Shakespeare play before the public sees it. I'm not exaggerating. Between time spent in class and time spent practicing lines and musical instruments at home, the hours add up to that mind-boggling figure.

The kids love doing Shakespeare, but their greatest joy comes from getting better at something over time and doing so in the company of friends. They begin in July, struggling to learn the summary of the play chosen for the year. Several months are spent listening to CDs and watching film versions of the production they will undertake. Finally, parts are assigned, followed by music instruction, intense choreography lessons, the blocking of scenes, and the creation of a sound and light design. No day is like the day before, and every rehearsal is better than the one preceding it. The children watch one another grow even within a ninety-minute session.

The important point is that in learning to delay the gratification of actually performing the show for an audience, the wisest kids discover happiness in waiting for the payoff. Suddenly, Nirvana is not something that has to be waited for at all. It's right there in front of them.

In an era when everything is sped up, teachers and parents might consider slowing things down. Take extra time working on a project at home, producing a play, preparing for a concert, or painting a school mural. Involve children in activities where the end is not even in sight at the beginning of the project. It is understandable that we constantly look for quick successes to make us feel better. Test scores and grades have seen to that. But the challenge is for our children to be successful long after they have left our classrooms and homes. If we adults can postpone our gratification and teach the children to delay theirs, the pot of gold at the end of the rainbow will no longer be merely a fairy tale.

## Game Over?

It was an exciting inning as the Dodgers almost made it happen, but they wound up losing, 8–6, and left the bases loaded. The Cardinals were just a bit better on this Friday evening. The kids clapped as both teams left the field.

I hoped some of the lessons taught at the game would stay with the kids for years to come. There are no guarantees. But if we make our best effort every day, we can help young people avoid the seemingly inevitable dumbing down that the world encourages. It is no surprise that I hear from thousands of people around the world who know the odds and continue to fight the good fight. Everyone who has raised children knows a child who has beaten the odds, accepted the challenge, and avoided the assembly line of mediocrity.

My students have been blessed to meet many such human beings, some of whom once sat in a tiny, leaky classroom called Room 56 and rose from there to great heights. Today many of those courageous kids have become the first members of their families to graduate college, going on to become environmental scientists, physicians, and journalists. And being extraordinary, they often return to the classroom where it all began to help other young children follow in their footsteps.

Fortunately, one such young lady named Joann wrote a college admissions essay about her journey through childhood for Northwestern University. In this chronicle of her young life story, little ones can see the possibilities that await them. As of this writing, Joann is studying for her doctorate in music, but her essay never mentions grades or test scores. Instead, she chose to focus on the important stuff. She wrote of many fond memories, but summed up what she felt was the most important thing she had learned being in Room 56:

> I was provoked to think.
> I was challenged to stay away from the ordinary.
> And I did.

Time will tell if our children will accept the challenge. But as long as we have time to give them, it's time well spent.

# Throwing Starfish

It was about eleven P.M. when the kids piled into the van and we headed for home. Truth be told, I was looking forward to some sleep and a couple of days off.

Even though most of the crowd had left, it still took quite a while to get the kids home. The radio in the van broadcast Dodger chat after the game, and the kids giggled as frustrated fans lambasted the manager, players, and anyone else they could think of while trying to lay blame for the evening's loss.

Jin Uk, the little professor, was the last kid dropped off. I watched him disappear into his old building and waved to his mom, who smiled a thank-you to me from her window.

Our school was only two blocks away, and I realized I had left some papers in the classroom. It was my own fault. After rehearsal, I had hurried the kids out the door, and made sure that Sammy, the little boy who had to be left behind, was all right. In doing so I forgot to take home the kids' essays, which I had said would be returned on Tuesday. It was a pain to go back to school, but a promise is a promise.

Stifling a yawn, I thought about starfish throwing. There is a legend that tells of a man standing on a beach, surrounded by thousands of starfish that have washed ashore and are dehydrating. The man picks them up, one by one, and casts them back into the ocean. A child walks by, puzzled by the man's actions.

CHILD: What in the world are you doing?

MAN: Well, I'm trying to save these creatures. They're dying.

CHILD: (seeing the task is impossible) Well, you're not going to save them all.

MAN: (picking up one) That's true, but I can save this one.

I hoped I had thrown a few starfish during the day.

Our school is locked up and alarms are set at 11:00 each evening. Jonathan, our night manager, does a fantastic job of leaving the campus ready for use when we return. My beloved principal has entrusted me with the keys to the school and the alarm codes. It would take a few minutes, but I would be able to enter the school and shut off the alarms before entering Room 56. A call to the school police informed them I was on the grounds, and I promised to call them back before resetting the alarms and leaving. It was a hassle, but Tuesday morning would be better with the kids happy to have their papers back.

It was quite dark as I ascended the stairs to Room 56, and then something scared the hell out of me. A voice from the darkness below:

SAM:   Rafe!

RAFE:  Jesus! Sam? You scared the hell out of me!

SAM:   Hi, Rafe.

RAFE:  What in the world are you doing here? It's mid-
       night!

SAM:   My mom didn't come.

RAFE:  But couldn't you call anyone? Couldn't anyone help
       you?

SAM:   It's okay. I figured you'd be back. I've been read-
       ing.

Outside on the playground, near the bottom of the stairs
that lead to Room 56, Sam had found a bench near one of the
dim playground lights. He had spent the last six hours reading
about the World War II campaigns of Patton and Montgomery
in Italy.

RAFE:  But Sam, it was just luck I came back. You could
       have been stuck here all night.

SAM:   But you did come back.

RAFE:  But it was just luck!

SAM:   But you did.

RAFE:  (too tired to argue) Let me give you a ride home.

SAM:   You know I live out of the district. It will take a
       while to get there.

RAFE:  It's okay. You hungry?

SAM:   A little.

RAFE:  Let's get you something to eat on the way home.
       Here's my phone. Call your mom. She must be wor-
       ried to death.

SAM: (getting into the car) Are you having class tomorrow?

RAFE: No, it's the holiday weekend, Sam.

SAM: Could you take me to the downtown library? I want to read more about Montgomery. I thought the movie *Patton* was unfair to him.

RAFE: What about the library near your home?

SAM: I've read everything they have. The downtown one is better. And Rafe?

RAFE: Yes?

SAM: Since we have Monday off, maybe we could go to the military cemetery. We could place a flag on one of the graves. What do you think?

A smile came to my face. Another starfish.

# Acknowledgments
## Mona Lisas and Mad Hatters

In Tom Hanks's charming 1996 film *That Thing You Do!*, a garage band called The Wonders from Erie, Pennsylvania, becomes an overnight sensation. As they prepare to sing their hit song on national television, Lenny, the guitarist, has a question for Guy, the drummer. Genuinely puzzled by their meteoric rise to success, Lenny asks his friend, "How did we get here?"

I was thinking of that scene the other night in Room 56. The kids had just rehearsed their production of Shakespeare's *The Merchant of Venice* on a Thursday during their Christmas break. The school was empty, but the children had happily worked hard for eight hours. The highlight of the day was the band putting the finishing touches on Van Halen's "Right Now," complete with haunting piano riffs and blistering guitar solos. Unlike the dazed and confused guitarist from *That Thing You Do!*, however, I know perfectly well how we got where we are, and I am forever grateful.

I am privileged to write books because my extraordinary publisher, Clare Ferraro, recognizes substance over style. My editors,

Wendy Wolf and Kevin Doughten, pick me up when I stumble and convince the world that I occasionally know a thing or two about kids. Bonnie Solow is by definition my agent but in reality my friend. I trust all of these people, and I cannot think of any higher praise to heap upon them.

But my books could never have been written without the help of all who came before. The original group of Hobart Shakespeareans, now in their thirties and raising families, taught me more than I ever taught them. They showed me what was possible all those years ago, and challenged me to stay away from the ordinary.

Sir Ian McKellen was the first believer. When my students grow up, I want them to be like him.

Thanks to all the patrons who followed Sir Ian. You generously create infinite opportunities for so many deserving children.

My inspiring teaching colleagues at Hobart Elementary School continue to fight the good fight on the worst of days. I am honored to work with such talented heroes. Over the last decade, this fellowship has extended to teachers all over the world. Thank you for all of your letters, gifts, and support. It means a lot.

Andy Hahn, Craig Housenick, Sarah Scherger, and Dan Ciarfalia are artists who turned my dreams into reality. Your expertise creates a glow in the children that radiates long after a Shakespeare production ends.

Joann, Frank, Elizabeth, Matt, In Yong, Hwi Yong, Joanna, Ji Yeon, Jeffrey, Rudy, David, Oscar, Eugene, Tracy, and Linda represent a cast of thousands of former students. I am forever in your debt for creating a magical classroom culture that cannot be described in a book. Thank you for reminding me that our days attending baseball games, visiting Shakespeare festivals, and making music meant something to you all.

Ye Rim, Jin Uk, Austin, Jessica, and Cesar have kept the fires inside Room 56 burning. You and your friends have blazed a trail for others that will continue to open doors tomorrow, and tomorrow, and tomorrow.

And for my first editor, Barbara: there can never be a bad day as long as you are here.

For all of the extraordinary people mentioned, I thank the Lord there are people out there like you.